R.W..

DE, CORK.

Steps & Steeples
CORK

URBAN HERITAGE SERIES 1

STEPS & STEEPLES

CORK

AT THE TURN OF THE CENTURY

COLM LINCOLN

O'BRIEN
PRESS

FIRST PUBLISHED 1980 BY THE O'BRIEN PRESS
20 VICTORIA ROAD RATHGAR DUBLIN 6 IRELAND
REVISED AND REPRINTED 1981

ISBN 0 - 905140 - 82 - 6
ISSN 0332 - 1886
URBAN HERITAGE SERIES

JACKET DESIGN: FRANK SPIERS
BOOK DESIGN: MICHAEL O'BRIEN
MAPS: ADRIAN SLATTERY
TYPESETTING: REDSETTER LTD., DUBLIN
BINDING: JOHN F. NEWMAN
PRINTED IN THE REPUBLIC OF IRELAND
BY A. FOLENS LTD.

FOR MY MOTHER

Contents

Acknowledgements

I would like to thank the staff of the National Library, Dublin, for without their cooperation and assistance this book could not have been produced. I have been greatly helped by the kindness and generosity of many others; in particular Mr. Tony McNamara, Cork City Architect, Mr. Tim Cadogan, Cork County Library and Mr. Nicholas Sheaff, Director of the National Trust Archive.

I would also like to thank Sr. Marcella Barry, Mr. Charles Nash and Mr. Patrick Thompson, all of Cobh, Mr. Joey Dwyer of Glenbrook, Mr. Diarmuid Ó Murchadha of Crosshaven, Br. Stanislaus Nelson of the North Monastery, Cork, Mr. Walter McGrath, also of Cork, the staff of the Cork City Library, the staff of the Berkeley Library at Dublin University, the Editor of *An Cosantóir*, Lloyds' Register of Shipping and the Naval History Library, Ministry of Defence, London.

For permission to use copyright material I wish to thank Mr. Tim Pat Coogan, *Magill Publications Ltd.*, Mr. John Montague, Mrs. Harriet O'Donovan-Sheehy, Mr. Seán O Faoláin and the Society of Authors as the literary representative of the estate of James Joyce.

A special acknowledgement is due to Anne and Declan O'Sullivan whose hospitality enlivened my frequent excursions to Cork. Other friends, Anthony Brabazon, Mary Fingleton and Mary Lincoln, were also of great assistance in the final rush to meet my deadlines. Above all, I would like to thank David Nolan who not only persevered in reading and advising on my script but who, in innumerable other ways, gave generously of his knowledge of Cork. For this help and encouragement I am indeed grateful.

Colm Lincoln

The Evolution of Cork

'A wide, beautiful valley, running from east to west, sheltered between lofty and grassy hills, along the crests of which are the groves and terraces of many pleasant villas; a silvery stream winding through the fields, now shadowed by the overhanging woods, and now emerging into the sunlight between sloping lawns and meadows; and, far down in the valley, tall spires and long tiers of grey houses on the shelving hillside — such was the first view I caught of Cork the beautiful.'[1]

The scene which William Bulfin described in 1907 is a fitting introduction to any account of Cork, suggesting as it does the snug and compact character of the place. It is a theme which recurs in other descriptions of the city. Daniel Corkery has referred to the way in which the 'odds-and-ends' of urban life are 'flung higgledy-piggledy together into a narrow double-streamed, many-bridged river valley'.[2] His one time pupil, Seán O Faoláin, having climbed high on the hills overlooking the city, described how Cork 'was threaded by channels; about us she was girt by praying spires; beyond, as to our hands, the small houses shoulder to shoulder, dimity-screened and dim, made steps-and-stairs of the hill'.[3]

The city takes its name from the marshy spot or *Corcaigh* which lies between a series of steeply rising hills, some miles to the north-west of the harbour. It was here on an island between the channels of the Lee that ships sought the safe haven to which the motto on the coat of arms of Cork refers — *statio bene fida carinis* ('a safe place for ships'). The harbour has played an important part in the development of Cork and, even today, ships are still moored close to the heart of the city.

It was the harbour that attracted the Vikings who founded a settlement at the head of the tidal waters of the Lee, sometime in the early ninth century. This settlement was situated in the low-lying area between the present North and South Gate Bridges, not far from the earlier monastic settlement with which St. Finbar is associated. His monastery is said to have been located in the area where St. FinBarres Cathedral now stands. However, it was with the Vikings (or the Ostmen as they were also called) that the commercial life of the city originated, and when Henry II divided the province of Munster amongst his followers after the Anglo-Norman invasion, he ensured that 'the city and the cantred of the Ostmen' were retained for the Crown.[4]

In the five hundred years or so that separated the reigns of Henry II and Charles II, Cork saw little change. Camden described it in 1586 as being 'of oval form, enclosed with walls and encompassed with the channel of the river which also crosses it'.[5] Along the length of the oval stretched North and South Main Streets with a dock dividing them at what is now Castle Street. When the city finally expanded beyond the walls in the late seventeenth century, it was to the high ground along Blarney Street and Shandon in the north and to the corresponding area around St. FinBarre's in the south. It was during this period that Cork's reputation as a centre of the provisions' trade was established; large quantities of butter and beef, as well as fish and pork, were exported to England and the Colonies.

Throughout the eighteenth century, trade

continued to flourish. By its close, barrels of beef and butter were being exported to places as far afield as New Zealand and Jamaica. The butter trade in particular is associated with Cork. Beginning in 1770 all butter coming into the city was graded according to its quality by inspectors appointed by a voluntary body known as the Committee of Merchants. The Cork Butter Market dominated the commercial life of the city well into the nineteenth century. Hundreds of men were also employed in the slaughtering of cattle and the export of beef and hides, while more were needed by the breweries and distilleries for which Cork is still noted. To the present day, commerce has continued to be more important than industry in Cork and, despite the large new industrial areas that have developed around the harbour, the city is still commercial and residential in character.

Over the years the marshes which lay to either side of the original city walls were gradually reclaimed, beginning with the north-east marsh which lay between Patrick Street and Lapp's Quay. Dunscomb's Marsh (between Patrick Street and the South Mall) and Dunbar's Marsh (Morrison's Island) were reclaimed during the late seventeenth and eighteenth centuries, as were Hammond's Marsh and Pike's Marsh which lay to the west. Cork however continued to be a city of waterways, and when Arthur Young visited it in 1776, the city seemed to him 'to resemble a Dutch town, for there are many canals in the streets, with quays before the houses'.[6] Many of today's streets were formed when these canals were later arched-over.

Cork, like Dublin, had its Wide Street Commissioners from 1765 on, but the nature of the terrain and a shortage of funds prevailed against any ambitions they may have had for expansive Georgian townscapes. As a result, the city retained its compact quality which, it could be argued, was better suited to the more assertive displays of architectural individuality which later generations seemed to prefer. The view from Patrick's Bridge in Cork has been compared, in a book by Mícheál MacLiammóir, to the romantic and impressionistic qualities of a Turner painting; whereas 'to look along the Liffey is still, despite the intrusion of a few functional cubes, like seeing an 18th century aquatint come to life'.[7] The analogies are apt, for though Cork retains some fine examples of its eighteenth century heritage, the city has little of the Georgian formality of Dublin.

Few of the eighteenth-century architects who built in Cork are well known. One of the most famous is the Sardinian, Davis Duckart. He designed a Mayoralty House at Grenville Place, but as the building later became a hospital, William Lawrence — whose photographs are used in this book — does not seem to have considered it of sufficient interest to merit a photograph. The best known of all Cork buildings, St. Anne's Shandon, is by John Coltsman; a local figure who deserves to be better remembered for he was also responsible for another former landmark, the leaning tower of Christ Church.

In the early nineteenth century architecture in Cork finally came into its own with the advent of the rival pairs of brothers, James and George Richard Pain, and Thomas and Kearns Deane. The Pains originally came to Ireland to supervise the building of Lough Cutra Castle, Co. Galway, which John Nash had designed for Lord Gort. The Deanes were a local family with less cosmopolitan connections, but, like the Pains, they had a long involvement in the building trade. When Alexander Deane, the father of Thomas and Kearns, died in 1806, his widow took over the business. She built the great Victualling Yard, or Naval Supply Depot, on Haulbowline, visiting the site by boat each day from her house on Lapp's Quay. Part of the work involved the building of a water tank which was capable of holding over a million and a half gallons; a feat which has not gone unremembered:

'But not forgetting Haulbowline Island
That was constructed by Mrs. Deane;
Herself's the lady that stowed the water
To supply the vessels upon the main.'[8]

Her sons continued building well into the Victorian period, although their last major work in Cork was University College, which was built between 1846-49. Benjamin Woodward, who assisted with the drawings, became a partner in the firm in 1851. Three years later they moved to Dublin. The 1850s marked an important divide for it was around

that time too that James Pain ceased to practice. His younger brother, George Richard, had died in 1838.

The reputation of these rival pairs of brothers has tended to overshadow the achievements of other architects and engineers, in particular Sir John Benson who was knighted for designing Dublin's Great Exhibition Hall in 1853. Benson seems to have been the archtypal Victorian with a capacity for work which must have astounded even his contemporaries. Hundreds of miles of road in east Cork were constructed under his direction, and after the great flood of 1853 he replaced no less than thirty-one bridges throughout the county. Other commissions included St. Vincent's Church and the Waterworks on the Lee Road; the latter being 'arguably the best example of industrial architecture in the city'.[9] Benson's greatest achievement, however, was the great railway tunnel under St. Patrick's Hill. The excavation of this tunnel produced a great deal of red sandstone which was used by the local building industry. The crumbling quality of the sandstone made it difficult to carve and as a result many sandstone buildings had their window and door surrounds cut from the more amenable local limestone. This contrast between red and white stone was obviously enjoyed for its own sake, and when the sandstone quarries closed at Tivoli in 1859 brick was used in its place. Even today the different coloured stonework makes a visual impact. One writer has compared the centre of Cork to 'a beached raft barnacled with red brick and limestone public buildings'.[10]

In the late Victorian period a host of architects were involved in building in the city, the more notable locals being Arthur Hill and G. C. Ashlin. A great deal of church building was undertaken and such internationally renowned figures as William Burges and Edward Welby Pugin have left their mark. Indeed, the physical location of the churches in both city and harbour is a constant reminder of the role that they held in the life of the community. The advantages of hillside sites were well utilized by church architects. Shandon's steeple and the triple spires of St. FinBarre's appear at the focal point of many city views. The early nineteenth century terraces at Monkstown are dominated by the work of Pugin and Ashlin. Cobh, which was a mere straggling village in the eighteenth century, is now best identified by its splendidly sited cathedral.

The towns along the harbour shore also share something of Cork's compact quality. Italianate and Gothic style terraces climb from the water's edge with an elegance and economy of space that has been rarely equalled. Many were built in the 1830s when Glenbrook and Monkstown took over from Passage as the principal resorts on the western side of the harbour.

Cobh, once a mere cove of Cork, developed in a more boom-town fashion, beginning in the late eighteenth century when the harbour became the chief port of assembly for convoys sailing to America and the West Indies. The Napoleonic wars saw the firm establishment of the Royal Navy in the harbour and the 'cove of Cork' became a town of some significance, with convoys of up to 600 ships lying off-shore waiting for wind. The town went into a brief decline on the withdrawal of the Navy in 1815, but by the late 1830s was well on the way to recovery and became a resort of sufficient respectability to justify a visit from Queen Victoria in 1849, 'so as to give the people the satisfaction of calling the place Queens-town'.[11] Despite the opposition of the Cork-dominated Harbour Commissioners, the town had some success in attracting the trans-Atlantic cargo trade. Frederick Engels, writing to Karl Marx in 1869, described how 'on Queenstown quay I heard a lot of Italian, also Serbian, French and Danish or Norwegian spoken'.[12]

Nevertheless, Cobh will always be remembered as an emigrant port; a place from where innumerable ships headed out between the points, where the very land 'seemed to beckon towards America'. Here on the hillside, 'high above the harbour, was the great Roman Catholic Cathedral of Pugin's building, richly adorned that the emigrant's last glance might rest on an imposing symbol of his faith. Was it the votive memorial' — one writer asked himself — 'of a fugitive and disappearing race?'[13] It was a pertinent, if uncomfortable question, and one which was answered in the affirmative for well into the twentieth century.

While emigration was not, of course, peculiar to Cork, it is significant that the population of the city hardly changed between the reign of George II and the Second World War; increasing from 74,000 in 1750 to 90,000 in 1946. Cork, like many other Irish towns, missed the Industrial Revolution. There are few pictures of the city at the turn of the century which have the assorted bric-a-brac of industry competing in the background for attention.

The photographs in this book are, in many respects, a testimonial to Victorian achievement, a visual record of the impressive works of the engineers and architects who built the railways and public buildings, the quay-sides and bridges, that contribute so much to the character of Cork and its harbour. The guidebooks of the period were not lacking in their praise of these and other developments nor, it would seem, were the inhabitants. Indeed, if we can accept the description that accompanied William Lawrence's own *Views of Cork, Blarney and Queenstown* there was 'perhaps, no urban population prouder of the city it inhabits than that of Cork'.[14]

The Lawrence Collection

In 1865, William Mervin Lawrence (1840-1932) opened a photographic studio in his mother's shop at 7 Upper Sackville Street, Dublin, where she had carried on a successful business in fancy goods and toys for some years. He joined the ranks of a well-established profession which, according to the Irish Census of 1861, provided employment for ninety-four men and seven women. Though his elder brother was already running a photographic gallery in Grafton Street, it was the studios in Sackville Street which were to become famous. William took over the sale and later the production of scenic photographs from his brother, and it was these 'Lawrence Views' which were to make the firm so well known.

Though the glass negatives are marked with the initials W.L., the photographs were in fact taken by the firm's employees. It was unlikely that a Victorian businessman would involve himself in such work. Moreover, William Lawrence had his right arm amputated while still a young man, eliminating the possibility of his being a photographer. The majority of the glass negatives, now known as the Lawrence Collection, have been identified by Kieran Hickey as the work of Robert French.[15]

Robert French (1841-1917) grew up in Dublin, where his father worked as a court messenger. As a young man he served for a time in the Irish Constabulary in Co. Wicklow, before taking up a career in photography in 1862. He began as a printer, the most menial position in a large commercial studio, but worked his way up through the profession. By the 1870s he was the photographer in charge of Lawrence's outdoor work. Around the same time, the first practical method of dry-plate photography was invented. Photographers working out-of-doors no longer had to carry all the paraphernalia for developing around with them. The scope of outdoor work was thus dramatically increased, and according to the Archbishop of York, President of the Dry Plate Club (1872), photography was now 'almost a child's toy'.

'Lawrence Views' were sold as lantern slides, as framed decorations for Victorian houses and hotels, and, beginning in the mid-1890s, as postcards. The expansion of commercial photography at the turn of the century owes much to changing Post Office regulations, which allowed postcards, as we know them today, to be sent through the mails. An immense number of new scenes were photographed in an attempt to keep abreast with demand. The Lawrence firm, if it was to remain competitive, had to extend its already large range of views, and the work of Robert French increased. By his retirement in 1914, he had spent over thirty years methodically and comprehensively photographing the entire country.

During the looting of Sackville Street in 1916, Lawrence's shop was set ablaze and the firm's records, as well as their valuable collection of portrait negatives, were destroyed. Luckily the glass negatives of the topo-

graphical views survived, and when William Lawrence died in 1932 the collection was still intact. Unlike some early negative collections which ended up in the walls of glasshouses, after the emulsion had been scraped off to make clear glass, the 'Lawrence Views' were purchased in 1943 by the National Library of Ireland; some 40,000 plates were bought for £300.

The photographs reproduced here are a representative sample of the firm's work in the Cork city and harbour area, and reflect the comprehensiveness and quality with which the Lawrence name was associated. The prints evoke both place and period with remarkable ease, though unfortunately no records with which to date the photographs have survived; this task has to be done by other means. The attempt to keep views up to date meant that an entire new series of plates was made whenever an important addition to the urban scene such as a new bridge or a tramway appeared. Besides being of interest in themselves, these details also facilitate the dating of some photographs.

While the photographic medium has a compelling mark of authenticity, one must nevertheless interpret its contribution to our understanding of the past with some caution. The 'Lawrence Views' were taken with publication in mind, therefore the acceptability of the prints was a matter of some importance. Victorian and Edwardian taste seems, not unnaturally, to have favoured those urban photographs which recorded the highpoints of local progress and achievement, such as views of public buildings and principal thoroughfares. Some views proved to be especially popular. St. FinBarre's Cathedral, Patrick's Bridge, and the seafront at Queenstown were photographed time and time again. It is noticeable, however, that Lawrence's carefully chosen subjects excluded the less savoury views, for few, then or now, would wish to purchase photographs of decrepit tenements or distraught emigrants.

Nevertheless, the overall atmosphere evoked in these pictures is not untrue of everyday life, for many, in late nineteenth century Cork. This book is intended to highlight that past, by bringing to a wider public the visual records of a heritage that is still remarkably intact.

Chapter 1
The City Streets

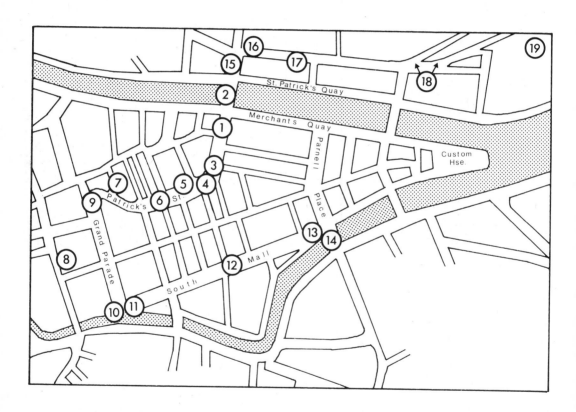

1. FR. MATHEW

The focal point of the city is the bronze statue by John Henry Foley (1817-74) erected by the citizens of Cork to the memory of Fr. Theobald Mathew, 'the apostle of temperance'. It was unveiled by John Francis Maguire, founder of the Cork Examiner, on 10 October 1864 and stands at the northern end of Patrick Street. In later years the tramway services radiated from 'The Statue' as did the fleet of new double-decker buses which replaced the trams in September 1931.

Fr. Mathew (1790-1856) was already well known in Cork for his work among the poor when he was asked by some Non-Conformist friends in the late 1830s to lead their temperance movement. His campaign was remarkably successful and within a few years the revenues from duties on spirits almost halved. The movement was not concerned exclusively with drink however. Rather, Fr. Mathew saw it as a means of tackling the wretched conditions in which so many people lived in pre-famine Ireland. He died, broken in health but still 'pledging' at Queenstown, in 1856.[16]

2. ST. PATRICK'S BRIDGE

'The smell from the river is something wicked, how do Father Mathew stick it? Here's up 'em all says the boys of Fair Hill.'

This refrain, from one of Cork's most popular songs, is just as applicable today as it was when this photograph was probably taken, around the time of the Cork International Exhibition, in 1902.[17] In this and other respects the scene hasn't changed remarkably and two well-known landmarks, namely Mangan's clock (left background) and Father Mathew's statue (centre), still remain. The arms of the city — a ship between two towers — can be seen on one of the quarterings of the flag flying from the building on the right. Patrick's Bridge was built in 1861 to replace an older structure which had been destroyed during a bad flood in November 1853. The new bridge was designed by Sir John Benson and is made of Cork limestone.

3. PATRICK STREET

VICTORIA HOTEL, CORK 624 W.L.

22

4. PATRICK STREET

The tram heading towards the camera is on its way to Summerhill. From 1901 until the early 1920s the trams used indicator boards and the vehicles on the Sunday's Well-Summerhill route has the same letters, W.S. (Western Road-Summerhill), at both ends of the car.[18] From December 1898 until September 1931, the Cork Electric Tramways and Lighting Company provided the city with both a tram service and electric lighting. The electric lighting subsidized the tramways which otherwise might have quickly gone out of business as had an earlier horsetram company which operated from 1872 until 1875.

The photograph of the Victoria was probably taken in 1898 as the standard for the electric tram is in position and apparently waiting for the wires. Though the hotel features in Joyce's autobiographical work *A Portrait of the Artist,* the twelve year old James actually stayed at the Imperial (see page 33) when he accompanied his father to Cork in February 1894 to sell the last of the family's mortgaged properties.[19]

5. EXAMINER OFFICE

In 1841, John Francis Maguire (1815-1872) founded the *Cork Examiner* whose offices can be seen in the three-storey building on the right. The *Examiner* was then an evening paper which was published three times a week with 'one great, one paramount object — the service of Ireland'.[20] At the time the *Examiner* took this to mean support for O'Connell's repeal movement, triennial parliaments, vote by ballot, and the disestablishment of the Church of Ireland. Maguire, a strict constitutionalist, represented Dungarvan in Parliament from 1852 until 1865 and Cork city from 1865 until his death. He was Mayor of Cork on four occasions and for his services to the Catholic Church created a Knight of St. Gregory. Maguire died in Dublin in November 1872. Under the direction of his surviving partner, Thomas Crosbie, the *Examiner* became a morning daily and two new papers were also launched, the *Weekly Examiner* and the *Evening Echo*. The *Examiner* is still a family business, and the Crosbies continue to play an active part in the running of what is now one of Ireland's oldest newspapers.

This scene was probably photographed in the early 1890s. The impact of the trams can be appreciated by comparing it with the photograph on page 22, which shows much the same view a decade later.

PATRICK ST. CORK. 589. W

6. PATRICK STREET

Patrick Street, along which the city's chief shops are ranged, sweeps in a broad curve along one of the former navigable approaches to the old city. The marshs which lay to either side were fully reclaimed and built on by the mid-eighteenth century. By 1830 the channel itself was completely covered over and today one of the few reminders of the former waterway is the position of some doorways which stand high up beyond a flight of steps; such as those on the left of this picture. An advertisement for 'Cook's Tours' can be partially seen on the gable nearby, while underneath there are posters for the rival Cunard and White Star shipping lines. Their liners called at Cobh, then known as Queenstown, on the way to America. The buildings in the background were burnt by rampaging Black and Tans and Auxiliaries on the night of 11 December 1920 following an IRA ambush at Dillon's Cross, some 200 yards from Victoria Barracks, earlier that day.[21]

7. SS PETER AND PAUL

After a 'memorable competition' in 1859, a design by Edward Welby Pugin was selected for this church which stands only a few yards from Patrick Street, on the site of the former Carey's Lane Chapel. According to one disappointed competitor, the selection committee was composed of retailers of soap, tea and whiskey, who knew 'nothing of architecture' and who were canvassed in a manner 'beyond comprehension'.[22] However the *Dublin Builder* thought highly of the design, if not of the site, which is 'so completely obscured that the stranger shall have . . . . difficulty in discovering what should be a prominent and conspicuous feature amongst the monuments of the city'.[25] Red sandstone from Glanmire was used extensively in the building, along with limestone, Portland stone, and marble for the more decorative work. The marble altar is by G. C. Ashlin.

8. CHRIST CHURCH

The Victorian opulence of SS Peter and Paul marks a decided shift from the tastes of an earlier age, which preferred the classical restraint of buildings such as Holy Trinity, Christ Church; seen here with its Georgian style pews and galleries still extant. The church, by John Coltsman, was erected in the 1720s to replace a medieval building which had been irretrievably damaged during Marlborough's siege of Cork in 1690. The tower and steeple of the new church were intended to rise to 170 feet, but when the builders were nearing 136 feet the foundations sank so badly that the tower had to be immediately reduced to 100 feet. For another hundred years the tower continued to lean to one side to such an extent that 'as crooked as Christ Church tower' became a local saying. Cork's answer to the Leaning Tower of Pisa was completely removed in 1828 and an Ionic portico by George Pain now stands in its place. In 1878 further work was again carried out and the apse, organ, and pulpit that we see here were erected.[24] Christ Church, which traditionally had been the city's civic church with pews for the Corporation and a canopy for the Mayor, was acquired by the Corporation in 1979 to house the Cork Archives Institute.

9. GRAND PARADE

'I sometimes wonder if the charm of Cork is not that it is a late-Victorian city
which has survived into our modern world. The bow fronts which undulate along
Patrick Street and the Grand Parade are redolent of a kind of contented charm.
If you long to be wildly contemporary such cosiness can be exasperating, but the
destruction of the world's major cities through overcrowding and crime makes
one value a city so compact that one can walk across it in less than an hour.'[25]

John Montague

10. GRAND PARADE

This photograph was probably taken in the early 1890s. The Berwick Fountain in the background was designed by Sir John Benson. It was 'erected in 1860 by Walter Berwick Esq. in remembrance of the great kindness shown to him by all classes in the city and county of Cork while presiding amongst them for 12 years as chairman of the quarter sessions.'[26]

> 'But mavrone! all the labour and money was lost;
> For it scatters the water that comes from its top,
> And 'twill wash down your shutters, thus saving a mop.
> When it works, try to pass it with shiny silk hat,
> And 'tis clear of the Fountain you'll keep after that.'[27]

The handsomely fronted building to the right of the fountain is the English Market. When it was first suggested that this meat-and-fish market should acquire such an elegant facade, one local wit proposed that the city motto *statio bene fida carinis* ('a safe place for ships') might be advantageously changed for that site into *statio bene fide carnis* ('a safe place for meat').[28] Closer at hand a carriage and pair are standing opposite the City Club. The building was extensively altered and refaced after designs by Sir John Benson in 1861.[29]

THE MALL. CORK. 581.W.L.

11. SOUTH MALL

The junction of the Grand Parade and the South Mall (seen here c.1890) has borne witness to the changing loyalties of the city's citizens. The Parade was once called *Sráid an chapaill bhúidhe* after the equestrian statue of George II by Vann Oss which stood in the middle of Tuckey Bridge — the site of the present Berwick fountain. When the waterway which then ran along the centre of the Grand Parade was covered over, George was transported to a spot overlooking the south channel; near the lamp on the right.[30] However, as both horse and rider were inclined to topple, a crutch was placed under the King's right arm and another beneath the belly of his charger. On the night of Monday, 3 March 1862 George's crutch 'mysteriously' slipped and the monarch, deprived of his prop, came to a sorry end.[31] Insult was added to injury when the Corporation was asked to sell the remaining part of the statue, namely the horse, so that both it and a newly manufactured King could be placed over Monsieur Hogini's circus in Mary Street. Despite the offer of 'the use of the bar' for the Aldermen, the temptation seems to have been bravely resisted.[32]

In 1906 an elaborate new monument by D. J. Coakley was erected nearby, at the end of the Grand Parade, 'through the efforts of the Cork Young Ireland Society to perpetuate the memory of the gallant men of 1798, 1803, '48 and '67'.[33]

31

SOUTH MALL, CORK, 1925. W.

12. SOUTH MALL

This scene was photographed either in 1899 or 1900, for during that short period the trams ran through Robert Street and Morgan Street from which the nearest tramcar is emerging. This route provided a short-cut from Patrick Street to the South Mall.[34] The building behind the trams is the Imperial Hotel. The houses to the left of the hotel, with first-floor entrances, are built of a yellow Dutch brick. The brick, which is identifiable by its colour and small size, was probably brought to Cork as ballast by ships which traded with Holland in the late eighteenth century. The next building, whose doorway is flanked by attractive lampstands, housed the Cork Gas Company. This building has a lot in character with the work of Richard Rolt Brash (1817-76), Cork architect and antiquarian.[35] The final house on the left, No. 71, was occupied by the National Bank, now part of the Bank of Ireland Group.

At the early age of nineteen, Thomas Deane was chosen to design the Commercial Building in the South Mall, now the Imperial Hotel. The Cork Commercial Buildings Company had been incorporated by royal charter in 1808 to provide an exchange where merchants could meet to discuss business and keep abreast of commercial developments abroad, via a newspaper library. The businessmen of the city were evidently well pleased with Deane's Neo-Classical design, for in 1816 he was asked to add a hotel and tavern to the rear of the building, in Pembroke Street (right). This became known as the Imperial Clarence Hotel. The original Commercial Buildings now form the main front of the present Imperial Hotel.[36]

13. SOUTH MALL

The South Mall is laid out on a grand scale, with a Georgian sense of expansiveness that one might more readily expect to find either in Dublin or Limerick. Dunscomb's Marsh (to the right) was largely reclaimed during the early eighteenth century and by the time Rocque's map of Cork was published in 1759, it had been built on as far west as Parnell Place. Dunbar's Marsh (Morrison's Island, to the left) was still being developed at this date and Rocque's Map shows a row of houses, or sites of houses, along the south side of the Mall. An open channel then rang along the centre of the street, but this was completely arched-over by 1832.

The former Provincial Bank, on the right, is positioned on a key site facing the river and makes an appropriate finish to what is Cork's most handsome street. By the time this photograph was taken around 1900, the South Mall was the undisputed centre of the city's financial and legal business.

14. PARNELL PLACE

Some interesting examples of Cork stone-work can be seen on the former Provincial Bank premises by W. G. Murray (left). The building is embellished with a great deal of sculptural decoration and, according to Séamus Murphy, the heads above the ground floor windows are 'not unlike those by Smith on the Dublin Custom House'.[37] The bank's rather ornate appearance would have been very much in vogue when it was built in the mid-1860s. The difference between this example of High Victorian Classicism and the simpler variety favoured in earlier years can be easily appreciated by comparing Murray's building with the Savings Bank of 1841-42 on the opposite corner. This was designed by the brothers Sir Thomas and Kearns Deane at a time when Neo-Classicism was already on the wane.

Anglesea Bridge was also built by the firm of Sir Thomas Deane and Company. It was replaced by a more elaborate swivel bridge in the early 1880s (see page 55) as the section which opened was considered to be 'much too small for the growing requirements of the shipping trade'.[38]

15. BRIDGE STREET

Bridge Street, as its name suggests, links Patrick's Bridge with the principal streets on the north side of the city. The tram heading towards Patrick's Hill is about to swing right into King Street, now MacCurtain Street, on its way to Summerhill. The clock on the right belonged to Barriscale's jewellery shop. In 1906 the premises beyond that were McNay's 'boot and shoe warehouse' (No. 4), Thompsons' confectioners (Nos. 2 and 3), and Hemsworth's pub (No. 1, at the corner). Part of the facade of Maddens — 'grocers and wine merchants' — can be seen on the left. No. 17 on the adjoining corner was a chemist's shop and facing it, at the corner of Coburg Street and Patrick's Hill, was Twomey's public house with the Beamish & Crawford sign.[39]

16. KING STREET

King Street has since been renamed MacCurtain Street in honour of Tomás MacCurtain. He had been O.C. of the Cork Brigade of the Irish Volunteers in 1916 and later became the first republican Lord Mayor of the city. He was killed at his home in Blackpool by a gang of masked raiders in March 1920. However, there was enough circumstantial evidence to show that the raiders had in fact been the police and the coroner's verdict was one of 'wilful murder' against Lloyd George, Lord French, Chief Secretary MacPherson, and other members of the Royal Irish Constabulary.[40]

The Irish Constabulary evolved in the 1830s as a centrally controlled police force which had responsibility for maintaining law and order throughout the country. Dublin had its own Metropolitan Police. Maintaining law and order was not an easy task and the Royal Irish Constabulary — the Royal prefix was acquired in 1867 — incurred a good deal of enmity, especially as they were called upon to help at evictions. Two members of the force can be seen in the foreground. Both the R.I.C. and the Dublin Metropolitan Police were replaced by the newly formed Civic Guard, as the Garda Síochána were first known, in 1922.

17. METROPOLE HOTEL

Miss Correll who, according to the poster in the window, 'will shortly open these premises' is first mentioned in Guy's street directory in 1903. She has since long gone, as have the Musgrave Brothers (to new premises) and the Newmarket Dairy. By 1980 only Lawsons Outfitters remained. The building was erected in 1897 and is a fine example of late Victorian hotel architecture with liberal amounts of plate glass and terracotta work at ground level. The red brick upper stories are broken by projecting bays and topped off by a steeply pitched, many gabled, roofline. A later extension to the east (left) in 1910 was attractively terminated with a corner turret, a characteristic feature of some Cork buildings of the period. The entrance to the Palace Theatre can be glimpsed on the right. This music hall was very popular, especially with the British military who, as Seán O Faoláin puts it were 'then garrisoned on us to the shame of our nationalists and the satisfaction of our shopkeepers'.[41]

18. CHURCHES AT GLANMIRE ROAD

The Catholic merchants of Cork continued to trade successfully throughout the eighteenth century and by the time of 'Emancipation' there seems to have been plenty of money for church building. St. Patrick's (1836) was the gift of the Honans, a wealthy Catholic family. It was designed by George Pain and was built in what was then a new suburb lying downstream of the old city. The interior was extensively remodelled in 1894.[42] The spire of the Presbyterian Church can be seen to the left of the portico.

A new Presbyterian Church was opened at the foot of Summerhill in July 1861, only a short distance from St. Patrick's.[43] At this stage the Gothic revival was well under way but, nonetheless, some members of the congregation seem to have felt uneasy about the design. At a dinner given for the workmen, the architect, Mr. J. Tarring, warded off possible criticism by arguing that while 'he would not for a moment advocate the employment of architectural forms for the purpose of introducing objects that would give to man the worship which was due only to God', he hoped 'the sternest would not object by and by to the introduction of a little ornamentation in the erection of ecclesiastical structure'.[44]

Though it is not so apparent in either of these photographs the upper reaches of the spire lean slightly to one side.

19. GLANMIRE STATION

If the great majority of Victorian buildings hankered back to the architectural styles of former centuries, there were some buildings such as railway stations and exhibition halls, which required large uninterrupted floor space, for which there was no adequate precedent. Some of the most innovative Victorian buildings, utilising new materials such as cast iron, were designed to solve these requirements. The Great Southern and Western Railway Station on Lower Glanmire Road, which was opened in 1893, is a fine example of close integration between architecture and engineering.[45] The track through the station had to be sharply curved in order to form a through connection from the Dublin line to the former Cork, Youghal, and Queenstown Railway which had been purchased by the GS&WR in 1866. The previous termini of both lines had been Penrose Quay (GS&WR) and Summerhill (CY&QR).

Chapter 2
Along the Quays

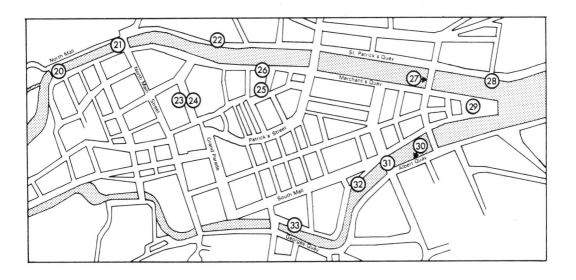

20. BACHELOR'S QUAY

Bachelor's Quay, where the 'shawlies' are walking on the right, was laid out in the first half of the eighteenth century when the marshy area to the west of the city walls was reclaimed. The Marsh, as it is still known, was then one of the more fashionable areas in the city but over the years the houses degenerated and many were eventually demolished by either private developers or by the Corporation during their slum clearance schemes. Among the victims was the Dutch-style 'Sheriff's House', more commonly known as the 'Doll's House', which featured in Frank O'Connor's 'The Saint and Mary Kate'. Of the houses we see here, the only one still standing is No. 24 Bachelor's Quay, whose fanlit doorway can be seen facing upstream.[46] Most of the houses on the North Mall, on the opposite side of the river, still remain.

21. NORTH GATE BRIDGE

After the great flood of November 1853 which destroyed St. Patrick's Bridge, the Corporation decided to replace the old North Gate Bridge by a new single-span structure.[47] The four piers of the old bridge had damned up the river and The Marsh was periodically flooded when the difference between the water level at either side of the bridge could be as much as four feet. Though the foundation stone of Sir John Benson's new bridge (below) wasn't laid until April 1863, it was opened for traffic within eleven months on St. Patrick's Day 1864. The ironwork, consisting chiefly of a graceful eight ribbed arch with a span of 106 feet, was prefabricated by Rankin & Company of Liverpool. The railings and lampstands were attractively ornamented and the external ribs of the bridge also elegantly decorated. The mouldings on the upstream side carried two medallions of Victoria and Albert while Daniel O'Connell and Thomas Moore were depicted on the other side. All told, it seems to have been a delightful piece of iconography and fairly representative of Irish sentiment at the time. In less than a century it had all gone and a much blander bridge was reopened on the site in 1961. Happily, the square still looks much the same, though the marvellous lampstand-cum-fountain has unfortunately been removed.

NORTH GATE BRIDGE, CORK. 2157. W.L.

ST. MARY'S CHAPEL. CORK. 2682. W.L.

R.C. CHAPEL. POPES QUAY. CORK. 5398. W.L.

22. ST. MARY'S CHURCH

This elegant church at Pope's Quay was gratuitously designed by Kearns Deane (1806-47) for the Dominican Friars. Prior to moving to Pope's Quay the friars had a house and church near the Butter Exchange in Shandon. The body of the new church was erected between 1832 and 1839, though the division of the interior into nave and aisles was not completed until 1861. The handsome Ionic portico also dates from 1861.[48] The exterior was originally intended to be a much more monumental affair, with a large central dome rising behind a Doric portico and flanking towers,[49] rather on the lines of St. Paul's Cathedral in London. The houses to the right have since been demolished and the insertion of a more recent building to their rear now obstructs the view of St. Mary's Cathedral, which is seen here framed between Shandon and the Dominican Friary.

Both the altar and its impressive canopy were designed by George Goldie. The canopy was erected in 1872, a year after the apse had been created by excavating the solid rock behind the sanctuary. The pulpit, also by Goldie, was 'erected by the exertions of the young men of the Sodality of the Angelic Warfare a.d. 1880'.[50] It is richly decorated with a wide variety of marble — Carrara, Sicilian, Siena, Galway Black, and Midleton Red. Fortunately, this interior with its Corinthian columns and coffered ceiling still remains; a worthy monument to the local plasterers who, conscious of their achievement, proudly 'paraded through the streets of the city carrying banners with the designs of this ceiling upon them'.[51]

23/24. THE COAL QUAY

'The Coal Quay — this is a part of the city amusing enough to strangers, yet far too unfashionable for the respectable citizens to take much interest in. The name seems a misnomer, as the place is some distance from the literal coal quay, and coal is not sold within its precincts . . . Chiefly on Saturday evenings the place is thronged with the poorer classes of tradespeople; and then, as the crowd surges along, the excited volubility of the several vendors becomes a study curious and amusing to the tourist. The 'merchants' frequently stand up on the counter, and express the several merits of their goods in praises replete with choicest native wit, and graced with the wildest blossoms of southern rhetoric.'[52]

Shaw's Tourists' Picturesque Guide, 1881

25. SCHOOL OF ART

The rapid growth of the city's trade led to the erection of a new Custom House in 1724 (building to right of tower). It faced a small harbour which has since been reclaimed and is now known as Emmet Place (formerly Nelson Place). When the Customs moved further downstream in 1814, the Emmet Place premises became vacant. In 1832 the building was acquired for a nominal rent by the Royal Cork Institution, a body founded in 1807 with the object of 'diffusing knowledge and the application of science to the common purposes in life'. Among its assets was a collection of casts, taken under the supervision of Canova, from antique sculpture in the Vatican. These had been sent by Pope Pius VII as a present to the Prince Regent, afterwards George IV, who was persuaded to present them to the Institution. The foundation of Queen's College in 1845 coincided with the closing of the Royal Cork Institution and in 1850 the building became a School of Design. As the costs of an extension by Arthur Hill in the 1880s were generously defrayed by a member of the Crawford brewing family, the school was subsequently renamed the Crawford Municipal School of Art.[53]

26. OPERA HOUSE

Following London's Great Exhibition of 1851, Ireland's first National Exhibition was held at Cork in 1852. The main exhibition hall, which was designed by Sir John Benson and stood on a site to the rear of the former City Hall, was subsequently offered to the Royal Cork Institution. Benson greatly altered and extended his original structure which was resurrected on waste ground adjoining the Institution's premises at Nelson Place. It was opened by the Lord Lieutenant, the Earl of Carlisle, on Wednesday, 23 May 1855.[54] Though the hall, which was then the largest in the country, was to be used for promoting the 'Fine Arts and Practical Sciences', the public's response was less than enthusiastic and by the late 1870s the former Athenaeum had been converted into the much more popular Opera House that we see here. According to Séamus Murphy 'when a Grand Opera Company came to Cork we talked about nothing else'. All the 'stonies' (stone masons) went 'and the apprentices were brought along on Saturday to the matinee'.[55] The building was destroyed by fire in December 1955 and has since been replaced by a new Opera House by Michael Scott, which unfortunately turns an immense blank wall to the river.

27. BRIAN BORU BRIDGE

The paddle steamer 'Albert', with an excursion pennant at the masthead, is about to go under Brian Boru Bridge. The Albert, 54-tons gross, was 140 feet long, 7 feet deep, and had a beam of 15 feet.[56] She was built in 1881 by MacIlwaine and Lewis of Belfast for the Cork, Blackrock and Passage Railway Company which competed with the Citizens River Steamers Company for the harbour trade. The River Company steamers went all the way up the Lee to the city, unlike the Railway's 'green boats' which normally stopped at Passage (from 1902 at Monkstown) where their passengers continued the journey by train to Cork. Brian Boru Bridge (1912) was part of a rail connection which linked Glanmire station to the Albert Street terminus of the Bandon and South Coast Railway. When river traffic was heavy 'a whole mass of regulations had to be observed' at the bridge 'where lift-men, barrier-men, water-men, and signal-men were employed'.[57] Some of the men stayed in living quarters over the road section on the right.

PATRICK'S QUAY, CORK. ... .W.L.

28. PENROSE QUAY

The steamship 'Killarney' was built at Dundee for the City of Cork Steam Packet Company[58] and in this picture is berthed opposite the company's premises at Penrose Quay. The building was designed by the Pains and is easily identified by its attractive Ionic portico. The company's dock workers suffered from bad working conditions, and Jim Larkin pointed out in 1908 that the firm was only paying its dockers in Cork 19s. 11d. a week, while in Liverpool it was paying 30s. a week. When the dockers successfully struck for better conditions that November, they got their first increase in wages for nearly twenty years.[59]

29. CUSTOM HOUSE QUAY

'The spreading Lee, that like an island fayre
Encloseth Corke with his divided flood'

Of the Elizabethan city, which Spenser described,[60] little survives, and for those approaching Cork from the quays these bonded warehouses give instead an indication of the city's nineteenth-century character. The rear of the Custom House can be seen in the centre background (above).

The Custom House was designed by Abraham Hargrave who died soon after the foundations were laid in 1814, leaving the remainder of the building to be completed by his son William.[61] The building is handsomely fronted but resolutely faces towards the city with scant regard for its magnificent riverside site. It can be seen here rising behind the funnels of the ship moored at neighbouring Lapp's Quay. The Royal arms on the typanum have since been replaced by the City Arms, carved by Michael Hutson.

EXHIBITION, CORK. 2780. W.L.

30. EXHIBITION HALL

Inspired by the success of the Great Exhibition of 1851 a number of Cork businessmen decided that Cork should host Ireland's first National Exhibition, the object being to 'elevate the moral and physical condition of the mass of the people, by the practical encouragement of native industry'. Temporary exhibition halls by John Benson were erected at the rear of the Corn Exchange on Albert Quay.[62] Among the numerous exhibits were 'beautiful specimens of the photographic art, with a daguereotype camera, and a machine on stand'.[63] These were entered by one of Ireland's first professional photographers, 'Professor' Leon Gluckman of Dublin. In 1890 the Corn Exchange was converted into a City Hall.[64] However, a new City Hall by Jones and Kelly now stands on the site as the previous building was destroyed by the Black and Tans in December 1920.

EXHIBITION. CORK. 2781. W.L.

31. PARNELL BRIDGE

Cork honoured one of its most famous parliamentary representatives by giving Parnell's name to this swivel-bridge opened in 1882. Only two years earlier, on Sunday, 3 October 1880, the people had shown their enthusiasm for Parnell in a demonstration which, in the opinion of Conor Cruise O'Brien, 'probably marked the climax both of the land agitation and of his own popularity as a semi-revolutionary leader'.[65] A two-mile long procession of labourers, tradesmen, and farmers had marched from Blarney into Cork to hear him reiterate his famous policy of moral coventry for land grabbers. This photograph was taken in 1883 as one of the posters on the hoarding refers to the Parnell Tribute which raised over £37,000 as a testimonial to him in that year.

32. THE 'ELLEN SUTTON'

The 'Ellen Sutton', a wooden brigantine of 190 tons, was built by Duneans of Prince Edward Island in 1868. She was registered at Cork and was owned by G. Sutton jr. whose family ran a coal-importing business from premises at the junction of the South Mall and Morrison's Quay, on the left. The ship was stranded on 11 February 1894 at Peterston Monmouthshire while on a voyage from Crosshaven to Newport in South Wales with a cargo of pitwood. At the time of her loss the ship's master was D. Farasy. The dimensions of the 'Ellen Sutton' were 105.3 feet in length, 23.5 feet in breadth and 12.7 feet in depth.[66]

33. HOLY TRINITY CHURCH

The Capuchins who founded Holy Trinity came to Cork in the mid-eighteenth century and settled in Blackamoor Lane near South Gate Bridge. In later years these premises were considered inadequate, and Fr. Mathew, who became Provincial in 1828, purchased the Charlotte Quay site (now Fr. Mathew Quay) for a new church and friary. Both the architect, George Richard Pain, and the Selection Committee wanted to build at Sullivan's Quay, a much more dramatic site at the southern end of the Grand Parade.[67] Work began at Charlotte Quay in 1832 but due to the expense of laying a foundation on the marshy site and other financial difficulties, the original design was considerably modified. Further lack of funds delayed completion of the truncated spire and cupola by Coakley until 1890.[68]

Chapter 3
Shandon to Montenotte

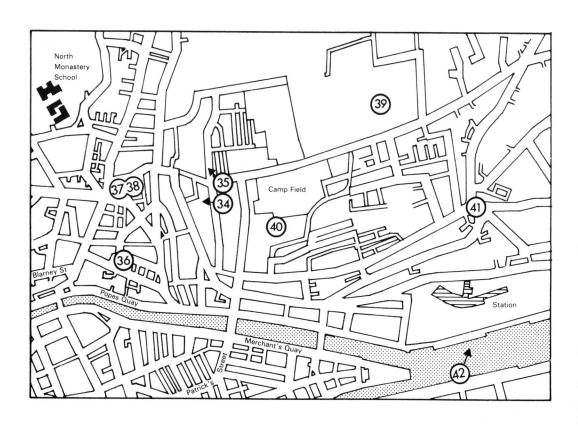

North
Monastery
School

39

37 38

35

Camp Field

34

40

41

36

Blarney St

Popes Quay

Station

Merchant's Quay

Patrick's Street

42

' Tis the bells of Shandon
That sound so grand on
The pleasant waters of the river Lee'

34. SHANDON AND BLACKPOOL

Shandon (left of picture) was the centre of the city's eighteenth century provisions' trade. Thousands of cattle were slaughtered here annually, and the meat packed into barrels for export. The blood from the many slaughter houses was the chief ingredient of the well-known local dish, 'drisheen'. It was here too that the butter trade was based, and the famous Committee of Merchants conducted their business in imposing splendour under the shadow of Shandon's steeple. The church's famous bells have been immortalised by Fr. Prout who now lies at rest in the adjoining cemetery.

35. BLACKPOOL

Throughout the nineteenth century the city continued to expand north-wards along the Blackpool valley. In 1854 James J. Murphy & Co. began to apply themselves 'with energy and enterprise'[69] to the manufacture of stout and porter at Lady's Well Brewery (chimney on left). The large building framed by the two chimneys in the centre is the North Presentation School and behind it, to the left, is St. Vincent's School. The chimney of the Peacock Lane Laundry can also be seen in the background and, on the hillside nearby, the pedimented facade of the 'North Mon'. The Christian Brothers moved their recently established school to this new building in the summer of 1818.[70] Sarsfield's Terrace, right foreground, was built by the Cork Improved Dwellings Co.[71] and makes a sharp contrast with the thatched cottages that lie beneath St. Mary's Cathedral at the other side of the valley (previous picture).

36. BUTTER MARKET

Some placenames along the old turnpike roads which lead to the city — such as *Carraig an Ime,* the Merchants Ford, and the Butter Road — give an idea of the former importance of the Cork butter trade. Butter came from as far away as Kerry to the Butter Exchange which was established in 1730 and managed by a Committee of Merchants from 1769 to 1925. A stringent system of inspection and classification established the reputation of Cork butter in the British and Colonial market as well as in continental Europe and America. By the end of the nineteenth century, however, it was being successfully challenged by butter from France and Scandinavia. The developments of 'Butterine', the forerunner of today's margarines, by the Dutch in the 1880s dealt a considerable blow to the Cork trade, and the 1890s were marked by both declining prices and sales.[72] The portico dates from 1849 and may be by Sir John Benson.

37. ST. MARY'S CATHEDRAL

In 1828 St. Mary's Cathedral, generally known as the North Chapel, was damaged by fire and subsequently the building was extensively renovated. The florid Gothic interior (opposite) is by George Pain. Sir John Benson was commissioned to design a new tower which, with its 200 foot spire, was intended to soar over the city.[73] However, the spire was never completed and Benson's tower (which is taller than that of St. Anne's Shandon) tended, in the eyes of contemporaries, 'to make the meanness of the church building more conspicuous'.[74] Benson was asked for further designs which would have doubled the size of the church, but as these were never implemented St. Mary's remained much as it was until the sanctuary was extended in the mid-1960s. The result of this latest addition is not very satisfactory; a poor compensation for the many sculptural works that were damaged in the process, including a statue of Bishop Murphy, the last known work by the Cork sculptor, John Hogan.[75]

38. ST. MARY'S CATHEDRAL

'About the mid-twenties, midnight mass was introduced in the Cathedral (or the North Chapel as it is sometimes still called) where my brothers and I were altar boys. It used to be a very impressive ceremony. The Cathedral Choir, of men and boys, was directed and conducted by the old maestro, Herr Fleischmann, father of Professor Aloys Fleischmann, and their singing was augmented by the Cecilian choir (drawn from the girls confraternity). The male choir sang from its usual 'enclosure' at the Gospel side of the altar and the female from the Gallery (now demolished) at the back of the Church. The synchronisation of the voices singing the usual Christmas hymns and carols was magnificent.'[76] *Jack Lynch, T.D.*

39. VICTORIA BARRACKS

Cork Barracks (renamed in honour of Queen Victoria at the turn of the century) was built to accommodate the large military garrison necessitated by the threat of the Napoleonic invasion. The principal buildings were designed by John Gibson and erected between 1801 and 1806. These and the other buildings that were added from time to time were ranged around three sides of a large parade ground. The Clock Tower Block was built in 1882. Most of the buildings were burnt by the anti-treaty Republicans in August 1923, after they learnt that Free State forces had landed at Passage. The barracks were subsequently rebuilt in much the same style and, apart from being renamed after Michael Collins, seems little different today.[77]

GOVERNMENT HOUSE.CORK.5736.W.L.

40. GOVERNMENT HOUSE

On a commanding site overlooking the very centre of the city stood Government House, a splendid example of Victorian fussiness which was rather unkindly described by one occupant as 'a large and needlessly ugly villa'.[78] The house was the residence of the Officer in Command at Victoria Barracks. Government House was destroyed in the early 1920s, presumably when the anti-treaty Republicans burnt the nearby barracks in August 1923, and was subsequently sold to a Mr. W. F. O'Connor who renamed it Mount Carmel. The house as rebuilt no longer retains the high-pitched gables and tower (left) which were once easily identifiable on the skyline as one looked up from the flat of the city.

41. ST. LUKE'S CROSS

The conical-shaped hut is one of Cork's few remaining toll-houses where farmers bringing livestock into the city paid a fee to the Corporation. The laying out of new roads and the building of St. Patrick's Bridge in 1789 diverted much of this traffic, and the area subsequently became one of Cork's more exclusive suburbs. In 1837 a Gothic chapel by the Pains was opened for the new residents and dedicated to Saint Luke.[79] By the mid-1870s, however, a larger building was required, and a Romanesque church by Sir John Benson and William Hill was erected on the site.[80] Following a fire in 1887 this second church was replaced by a new building (right) again by William Hill;[81] Benson had died in 1884.

42. ST. LUKE'S AND MONTENOTTE

'Oh, but any winter evening, stand on Montenotte, in the bay of some cosy bourgeois house, and look down through the battered wind-rattling window at the rain-washed town, and the spars of the ships on the quay shining in arc-light, and you can recapture easily the maritime quality of Cork.'[82]   *Seán O Faoláin*

Chapter 4
St. FinBarre's to Sunday's Well

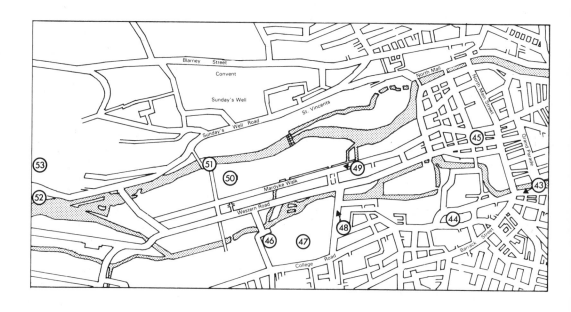

Blarney   Street

Convent

Sunday's Well

St. Vincents

Sunday's   Well   Road

North Mall

North Main Street

Grand Parade

53

51

50

Mardyke Walk

49

45

43

52

Western Road

48

44

46

47

Barrack   Street

College   Road

43. ST. FINBARRE'S CATHEDRAL

Despite the impending threat of disestablishment, the Church of Ireland community in Cork displayed what Jack Lynch has called a 'manly spirit of self-reliance' and having decided to erect a new Cathedral carried on regardless, building 'on a grand scale and to the highest standards'.[83] St. FinBarres was designed by William Burges for a competition in 1862 and built between 1865 and 1876. It is an architectural tour de force with a splendid set of spires which can be seen from many parts of the city (see page 71).

Burges's design met with bitter opposition from disappointed competitors and for a while even legal action was threatened. His detractors pointed out that he failed to provide a Chapter House; that his design could not seat a congregation of 700; and that it contained a 'grave structural defect in the arrangements for supporting the central tower'. The Cathedral's twelfth-century, French appearance was considered out of character with the reformed faith and 'highly unsuitable for the services of a Protestant church'. The principal objection was that the competition rules only allowed for costs of £15,000 whereas Burges's design would cost at least £30,000. Burges was unperturbed and retorted that 'no cathedral in the proper sense of the word was ever known to be executed for under £15,000'.[84] In fact the total cost almost came to what was then a staggering £100,000.

44. ST. FINBARRE'S, WEST FRONT

The west front of St. FinBarre's as it appeared after the scaffolding was removed and later when the sculptural ornamentation was completed (right).

73

45. THE COURTHOUSE

The Courthouse (1835), by the brothers James and George Richard Pain, was built in what was then a new street running westwards from the Grand Parade. The guidebooks of the period invariably quoted Macaulay's comment that the building's immense Corinthian portico 'would do honour to Palladio'.[85] However, the interior of the County Court section 'drew no admiration from those who had to conduct business there' and the Grand Jury (the antecedent of the present County Council) was faced with the expensive and lengthy task of carrying out piecemeal improvements.[86] The interior was completely destroyed by fire on Good Friday, 27 March 1891, but the magnificent portico survived.

46. THE JAIL

Around 1818 the brothers James and George Richard Pain were commissioned to design a number of new buildings at the old County Jail.[87] The most important of these was the House of Correction which was based on a radial plan with three wings of prison cells projecting from the central block. The Pains were at their most successful in designing the formidable looking entrance portico. This fine example of Greek Revival architecture was composed of a number of simple geometric shapes, with a minimum of decoration to distract the eye from the relationship of the various parts. While it never enjoyed a great success in Ireland, the style's severity was considered particularly appropriate for courthouses and prisons.

The Jail has since been acquired by the adjoining University, and the buildings which formerly rose from behind the portico and which were generally considered to mar the overall effect were demolished in the 1950s. Regrettably, the new University buildings that replace them are even less in sympathy with their surroundings.

47. QUEENS COLLEGE

The University buildings in Cork are probably the most successful example of nineteenth century University architecture in the country. They were designed by Sir Thomas Deane, assisted by Benjamin Woodward. The main buildings were ranged around three sides of a quadrangle, with the lecture rooms on the west side (left); the towered entrance, examination hall, and library on the north; and the residents of the President and Vice-President on the east. The president's garden, which lay behind the wall on the right, has since been opened to the students. The east and west wings are now totally given over to administration.

The college opened in 1849, but as late as 1903 a guide book pointed out that 'as the "godless" colleges have never found favour with the Roman Catholic authorities, Queen's has never attracted a great number of students'.[88] The establishment of the National University of Ireland in 1908 effectively overturned the original concept of providing an undenominational education, and University College subsequently flourished as a de facto Catholic institution.

QUEENS COLLEGE. CORK. 1946. W.L.

48. COLLEGE ENTRANCE

The contract for an entrance (left) to Queen's College was awarded to E.
Fitzgerald of Cork in 1879. The work involved not merely a new gate and bridge
but also necessitated the construction of an approach road which was to sweep
up to the front of the college.[89] Prior to this the main entrance was from the Jail
Walk, but as both staff and students apparently objected to 'sharing an entrance
with common criminals'[90] a new gate and bridge were built near the present
junction of the Western Road and Donovan's Road. When this photograph was
taken, the Western Road was as yet undeveloped. Donovan's Bridge which now
crosses the channel in the centre foreground was built in 1902. Amongst the more
prominent buildings at Sunday's Well in the distance are the Good Shepherd
Convent (left) and St. Vincent's Church (right). St. Vincent's was begun in
1851 to the designs of Sir John Benson. However, funds were slow in coming and
the building was not finished until 1886 from new plans by S. F. Hynes.[91]

49. MARDYKE WALK

'The leaves of the trees along the Mardyke were astir and whispered in the sunlight. A team of cricketers passed, agile young men in flannels and blazers, one of them carrying the long green wicketbag. In a quiet bystreet a German band of five players in faded uniforms and with battered brass instruments were playing to an audience of street arabs and leisurely messenger boys. A maid in white cap and apron was watering a box of plants on a sill which shone like a slab of lime-stone in the warm glare. From another window open to the air came the sound of a piano, scale after scale rising into the treble.'[92]

James Joyce

MARDYKE WALK, CORK, 6654, W.L.

50. EXHIBITION GROUNDS

The Cork International Exhibition was formally opened by the Earl of Bandon and the Lord Mayor of Cork, Alderman B. Fitzgerald on Thursday, 1 May 1902. 'Considerably over 10,000 persons passed the turnstiles on the occasion of the imposing inauguration ceremonial and the consequent financial result was', according to the *Cork Examiner,* 'eminently satisfactory'.[93] The exhibition grounds stretched for three quarters of a mile along the site of today's Fitzgerald Park and included bandstands, sports grounds, and various pavilions such as the Industrial Hall (above) where 'a magnificent effect was produced by the arrangements of electric lights around the cupola and dome'. On a more sober note the *Examiner* hoped that the exhibition would foster 'the few industries that remain in the country' and more particularly that the citizens of Cork would 'reap the benefits of having their city as the site of this temporary emporium'.[94]

Just behind the Industrial Hall was the Water-Chute, which proved to be one of the most popular attractions at the exhibition when it finally went into operation after a number of delays. It achieved a certain notoriety when a carpenter jumped from the top into the river below, a distance of 70 feet. He was rescued by the Sunday's Well ferryman and, apart from the shock, seems to have escaped injury. The *Examiner* disapprovingly noted that 'the affair is said to have arisen over a wager'.[95] The more normal course of descent was by boat.

51. SUNDAY'S WELL

The well-proportioned spire of St. Mary's Shanakiel (background) is a conspicuous landmark in the picturesque suburb of Sunday's Well. The Church was designed by W. H. Hill and consecrated in 1879.[96] The buildings in the foreground are older, and the bricked windows of the Georgian house to the left give it an attractive Gothic appearance. In 1927 Daly's bridge was erected on the site of the old ferry.

52. THE WATERWORKS

The waterworks which lie to the west of Wellington Bridge (now Davis Bridge) are by Sir John Benson. They were erected in 1888 and are a particularly fine example of the way in which different coloured materials can be used to enliven architecture. The 'streaky bacon style', or structural polychromy, became very popular in the late Victorian period, especially in Cork where plentiful supplies of different coloured stone were readily at hand.

The towers and gables in the distance belong to the Asylum. Despite opposition by cost-conscious local authorities, a government-inspired 'Cork District Lunatic Asylum Bill' received the Royal assent in August 1845. Local officialdom had its revenge, however, for the Board of Governors decided to call the new complex the Eglinton Asylum in dubious honour of Lord Eglinton, the Lord Lieutenant. The honour, it is said, did not meet with Eglinton's unbounded approval.[97] The Asylum, designed by William Atkins, originally consisted of three detached blocks built of rubble masonry 'with high-pitched roofs, gables and pointed arches everywhere'.[98] When further accommodation was required in the 1870s the obvious solution of building up between the blocks was adopted.

53. THE ASYLUM

'To minister to a mind diseased is, indeed, a noble charity, and, unfortunately, in Ireland there is great need of it. The continued political disasters of the country, and the disquieting social condition of the majority of the people, supplemented by very general distress, have had an injurious effect on Irish mental conditions. Lunacy, according to government statistics, has been decidedly on the increase of late years. Some English writers, oddly enough, have attempted to account for it on the ground that the Irish people, who formerly drank milk almost exclusively at their meals, have become confirmed tea drinkers — almost as much as the Russians. The Irish themselves laugh heartily at this English theory, and say it is not tea, but British rule, that is making them mad. The Cork Asylum, as shown in the sketch, fronts on the river Lee, and is otherwise pleasantly situated. It contains, at the present time, about a thousand inmates, many of them lunatics of a mild type, who, in their rational intervals, fully appreciate the comfort of their surroundings.'[99]   *Ireland in Pictures, c.1890*

Chapter 5
Carrigrohane and Blarney

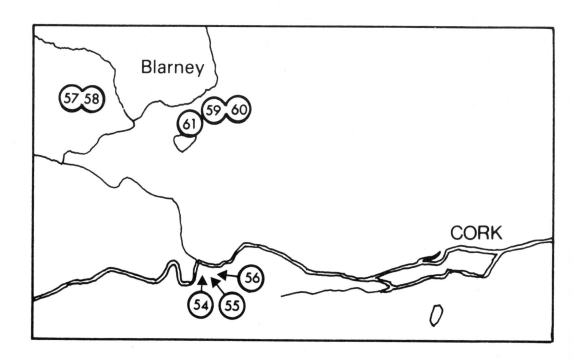

54. CARRIGROHANE CASTLE

This castellated house incorporates part of an older castle and is dramatically positioned overlooking the Lee only a few miles to the west of the city. The Carrigrohane Railway Stop (page 86) was located directly underneath. The original building was successively owned by the Barret, Wallis, and Hoare families and lay in ruins for many years before being converted into the present nineteenth century house.[100]

55. CARRIGROHANE RAILWAY STOP

Locomotive No. 7 of the Cork and Muskerry Light Railway waits at Carrigrohane Railway Stop. The Muskerry Tram was one of the more financially successful of the light railways constructed under the provisions of the Tramways and Public Companies (Ireland) Act of 1883. It tapped the valuable tourist traffic to Blarney Castle, although the route was longer and more circuitous than by the main road through Blackpool. Other branches of the railway extended to Coachford and Donoughmore. The advent of motor transport led finally to its closure in December 1934.[101]

56. CARRIGROHANE BRIDGE

This attractive skew-bridge at Carrigrohane was designed by Sir John Benson as part of a new approach to the city from the west.[102] The Ordnance Survey maps of 1841 show the line of the proposed new route, and the site of the bridge is indicated at the northern end of a mill-race, only a short distance from where it joins the Lee. The bridge consists of six limestone arches which stand, one behind the other, at an oblique angle to the stream.

57. ST. ANNE'S HYDRO

In the mid-1850s 'Dr. Barter, who had a hydropathic establishment at St. Anne's hill near Cork, constructed the first hot air bath that existed in these islands since the Romans held sway in Britain'. Though his project initially met with opposition, by 1875 the Dublin University Magazine was able to report that 'the salubrious and sanative properties of hot air are now appreciated by the medical profession'.[103] More than hot air was provided, however, and the establishment also contained a library and reading-rooms, a croquet lawn for the ladies, a river full of trout and salmon, hunting in the winter, and several billiard and bagatelle tables. The object of St. Anne's was both 'to restore good health and to promote cheerfulness and good temper'.[104]

58. TURKISH BATHS

In July 1870 a new Turkish Bath was opened at St. Anne's on a terrace below the main building. The flooring throughout was in red marble. The intended oriental effect was to be further achieved through a combination of mirrors, stained glass and rich tapestry. The pièce de résistance of the cooling room was a marble fountain and plunge bath, whereas 'special arrangements' were made 'in the hotroom for illumination by gas'.[105]

59. BLARNEY CASTLE

Blarney Castle was by far the most popular of all Irish castles, and every guidebook contained stories of its famous stone. By the end of the century the castle had acquired the status of a national shrine and, along with the ubiquitous round tower and ancient high cross, became an emblem of a newly discovered Irish Ireland. Not surprisingly, the centre-piece of the 'Irish Industrial Village' at the World's Columbian Exposition at Chicago in 1893 was a copy of the castle with a staircase leading visitors to the top where they could 'kiss the magic stone'.[106] Perhaps appropriately, 'Eire go braghery' and Blarney went hand in hand.

Apart from this, the castle is quite significant in its own right. It was built in 1446 by the McCarthys of Muskerry and consists of an enormous keep, with the remains of an eighteenth century Gothic mansion attached to one side. This later extension was added by the Jefferyes family who also laid out the elaborate landscape garden known as the Rock Close.

PEEP HOLE, BLARNEY. 1914. W.L.

60. THE BLARNEY STONE

'There is a stone there, whoever kisses;
    Oh! he never misses to grow eloquent,
    'Tis he may clamber to a lady's chamber,
    Or become a member of Parliament

A clever spouter, he'll sure turn out, or
    An 'out-an'-outer to be let alone;
Don't hope to hinder him, or to bewilder him,
    Sure he's a pilgrim from the Blarney Stone.'[107]

Fr. Prout

61. BLARNEY MANSION

In 1874 the Jefferyes family, who owned Blarney Castle, built a new mansion on a site overlooking the lake. It was built in the fashionable Scottish Baronial style and has certain affinities to similar buildings by the Ulster architect, William Henry Lynn. This was 'the golden age of Victorian countryhouse building' with 'industry and agriculture booming and British prestige at its height'.[108] In Ireland any faint rumbling of the incipient land war 'could only have been foreseen by a great leap of the imagination'.[109] Within a few years all had changed utterly, for a combination of bad weather, disastrous harvests, and falling prices culminated in a bitter and long drawn-out campaign against the land system on which the 'Big House' depended. Even in England, where the landlords retained an unchallenged position on their great estates, things were not the same after the agricultural slump of 1879-94. For as Lady Bracknell says in Wilde's *The Importance of Being Earnest*: 'what between the duties expected of one during one's lifetime and the duties exacted from one after one's death, land has ceased to be either a profit or a pleasure.'[110]

BLARNEY MANSION.
CO.CORK.2963.W.L.

Chapter 6
The Marina to Monkstown

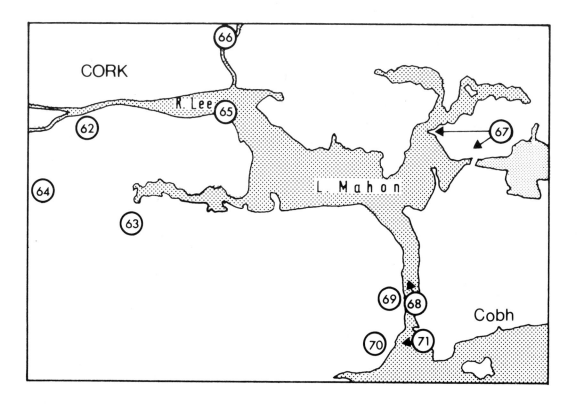

62. THE MARINA

This fine double row of elms was planted about 1856 by Professor Murphy of Queen's College. The embankment on which they stand — originally called the New Wall, later the Navigation Walk and now The Marina — was built from mud and gravel dredged from the river in the latter half of the eighteenth century. The slobland to the south of the embankment was gradually reclaimed and became a park which was used as a racecourse from 1869. Here 'young ladies and rebuilt older ones' searched for a tip or a husband while 'others full-chested and keen on any starter' paraded with parasols, velvet hats and 'flounces to entangle passing eyes'.[111] No longer do jockeys envisage 'champagne and an immortal hour' at the Park Races,[112] for in 1917 a sizeable portion of the park was sold to Henry Ford as the site for a factory where an altogether different breed of animal could be turned out — the Fordson tractor.[113]

63. DOUGLAS VILLAGE

'A tram ploughed by, shrieking and swaying, its top deck empty and rain-swept; its wall of glass dim with the passenger's breath, and it threw up a solid sheet of muddy water at either side as it passed!'[114]

Frank O'Connor

64. FR. MATHEW'S GRAVE

A simple cross marks the grave of Fr. Mathew in St. Joseph's Cemetery, a burial place which he himself established (in the grounds of the former Botanic Gardens) so that, as Thackeray put it, 'Protestants and Catholics might lie together without clergymen quarelling over their coffins.'[115] Prior to the acquisition of St. Josephs in 1830, the only graveyards available to Catholics belonged to the Established Church and there were occasional episodes of religious bitterness when Catholic priests sought to exercise their ministry in them. This problem was rectified in St. Joseph's by religious segregation. The whole affair was an apt, if unfortunate, illustration of what one of Ireland's greatest historians saw as the failure of the various churches; for as William Lecky ruefully observed, 'if the characteristic mark of a healthy christianity be to unite its members by a bond of fraternity and love, there is no country in the world in which christianity has more completely failed than in Ireland'.[114]

65. BLACKROCK CASTLE

The promontory where Blackrock Castle stands was first fortified by Lord Deputy Mountjoy during the reign of James I. In the early eighteenth century the Corporation built an elegant domed octagon on the site where the Mayor gave an annual summer entertainment in his capacity as Admiral of the Harbour. This building was destroyed by fire in 1827, and the Pains were subsequently commissioned to design the castle that we see here.[117] When Queen Victoria visited Cork in 1849 she stopped on her way upstream and, as she noted, received 'a salmon and a very pretty address from the poor fishermen of Blackrock'.[118] Her son, Edward VII, also received a salmon on a later royal visit, but on this occasion there was no 'pretty address' and instead the salmon was brought by a private steam launch to the royal yacht at Queenstown.[119]

66. GLANMIRE

'The wild flower blossoms early in summer
such nature can never consume:
I'm blessed you will stay there for ever
with the horsechestnuts covered with bloom.

But now on a fine summer evening,
When you are in full leisure time,
Walk out the lower road from Cork city
and view the fine Groves of Glanmire.'[120]

67. FOTA

In the middle of the last century James Hugh Smith-Barry laid out formal gardens behind his house on Fota Island. Though the parterre has since been grassed over, the arboretum which he began was continued and it now has an international reputation.[121] The house itself had been greatly extended around 1820 by the fashionable father-and-son practice, Sir Richard and William Vitruvious Morrison. The addition of two-storey projecting wings provided the basis for a wide-spreading Regency mansion whose simplicity gives little indication of the riches within.

A battlemented folly by John Hargrave stands at the very tip of the island only a short distance from where the Cork-Cobh railway cuts through the demesne. From here the woods and parkland roll eastwards until they are finally enclosed by the great wall, which adjoins the main road, as it curves along the far side of the island. The estate was sold to University College Cork in 1975.

FOTA.CO.CORK.2691.W.L.

FOTA CASTLE.CO.CORK.2690.W.L.

MONKSTOWN. Co. CORK. 2778. W L

68. GLENBROOK AND PASSAGE WEST

As one looks upstream from Rushbrooke, the Royal Victoria Hotel and Baths can be seen on the left and, away to the right, the masts of ships at Passage. They mark the end of the natural deep-water channel, and in 1800 the ruling depth between there and Cork was only three feet. As a result many ships unloaded at Passage and in 1832 a dockyard was established, which was renamed the Royal Victoria Docks in 1849 in honour of Queen Victoria. It seemed likely for a while that both Passage and Queenstown might syphon off some of the city's port trade. However, the Cork-dominated Harbour Commissioners reacted to the threat by starting serious work on the dredging of the river. A powerful dredger and river barges were constructed under the direction of Sir John Benson and by the time this photograph was taken at the end of the century, a depth of fourteen feet had been achieved. As a result, Passage fell on very bad times and even the docks which bore Victoria's name suffered badly from competition from English yards.[122]

69. GLENBROOK

In 1810 Passage was described as a 'small, but bustling town' which was 'much more convenient for travellers and sea-bathing, than either Cove or Monkstown', though it was 'much in want of a few bathing machines'.[123] As the town became increasingly industrialised, however, the holiday makers and more affluent residents moved southwards towards Glenbrook and Monkstown. By the 1850s the social divisions were fairly clearly drawn and Passage's rows of Dock Cottages had their counterpart in such middle-class housing schemes as Glenbrook Terrace (above).

The Royal Victoria Hotel and Baths possibly date from sometime in the early 1800s[124] though the name itself is obviously of a later vintage. It was a 'curious structure' which, according to one popular guidebook, was 'suggestive of the primitive lake dwellings of the age when "wild in woods the nobel savage ran" '.[125] Nonetheless, the hotel was 'a very comfortable place of residence', and the baths were easily accessible by train from Cork. After the extension of the railway to Crosshaven in 1904 the baths fell into disuse and now all that remains are the outer walls of the lower building on the left.

70. MONKSTOWN CASTLE

Monkstown Castle is one of the best-preserved examples of the great gabled houses that were generally built in Ireland during the early seventeenth century. While their symmetrical layout and use of decorative detailing indicate the influence of Renaissance ideas, these buildings were still strongly defensive in character. They usually consisted of a rectangular living block which was flanked with protecting towers at each corner. The castle at Monkstown was built by Anastasia Archdeacon (née Goold) in 1636. Story has it that she intended it to be a surprise for her husband when he returned from serving in the Spanish Army. He is rather ungenerously credited with disliking the end result, even though the total cost is reputed to have only come to four pence after Anastasia had charged the workmen for their food and lodging. As it turned out, the Archdeacons did not enjoy their new castle for long. It was granted to Captain Thomas Plunkett of the Parliamentary Navy in 1647. He in turn was replaced and a succession of owners followed before it was sold to the Shaw family in the late eighteenth century. They vacated the castle in 1869, and it has lain in a neglected state ever since.[126]

71. MONKSTOWN

Monkstown is situated at the point where the river opens on to the lower harbour. The church by E. W. Pugin and G. C. Ashlin (right) is well positioned on the hillside, overlooking the semi-detached and terraced houses which rise in tiers from the water's edge. The paddlesteamer at Monkstown Pier is probably on its way upstream to Passage where the passengers could take the train to the city. Nearer at hand, two sailors are working on the fore-top and yard-arm of a three-masted barque which is moored at Rushbrooke.

Chapter 7
Queenstown

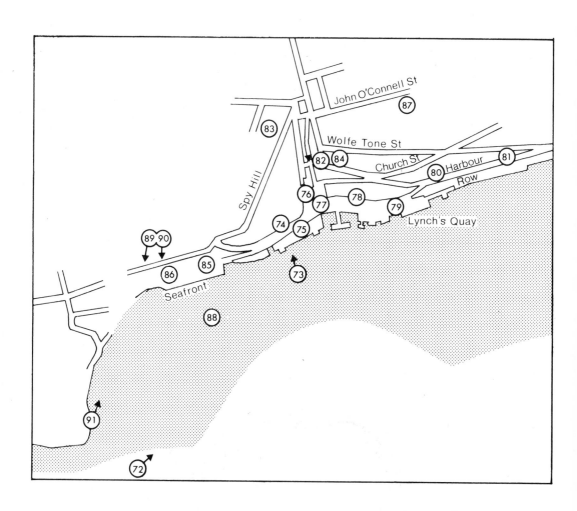

72. QUEENSTOWN

'Seen from the water, Queenstown, with its dominating but towerless cathedral, is very attractive. The town is built in terraces on the hillside, rising rank behind rank and all commanding a fine prospect across the harbour. The harbour itself, whether seen from the deck of a steamer, or from the heights above the town, makes a majestic picture. A modern warship is generally moored as guardship off the town, but even such vessels as the 'Howe' [right] look mere buoys on that vast expanse, while gun-boats and torpedo boats are no better than corks. The whole British navy could find comfortable anchorage here and there would still be room for an enemy's fleet if one cared to come . . . Queenstown was formerly known as 'Cove', its present name arising from the fact that Queen Victoria landed here on her visit to Ireland in 1849. Apart from its importance as a port of call for the American liners and as a great naval and military station, Queenstown is rapidly acquiring a reputation as a health resort, particularly for the winter.'[127]   *Guide to Cork and the Southwest, 1903*

73. WESTBOURNE PLACE

The western end of Cobh contains some fine examples of the sort of housing which have made it — at least in an architectural sense — 'one of the best "small towns" in these islands'.[128] The Italianate style of architecture was particularly popular in early Victorian seaside resorts, and even today Cobh still conveys a sense of grandeur which is quite different from most other Irish towns.[129] Cobh, or Queenstown as it was called from 1849 to 1920, was where the Royal Cork Yacht Club was based. The former clubhouse (left) has been attributed to Salvin.[130] This prestigious club, which dates from 1720, amalgamated with the younger and more vigorous Royal Munster Yacht Club in 1966 and now operates from Crosshaven. Apparently the Methodists have also left Cobh, for by the late 1970s their elegant church with its tall Corinthian portico and slender cupola, had been converted into a discotheque. The two-storey villa on the hill once housed the United States consulate. A host of other countries were also represented in the port; ranging from Russia to Peru and including such former luminaries as the Ottoman Empire and the 'Secretary of State for India in Council'. Most of the thirteen-house crescent can be seen on the right, while beneath, a handsome series of stucco-fronted buildings stretch along Westbourne Place.

74. QUEEN'S HOTEL

Efforts by the local medical fraternity to boost the town's reputation as a health resort seem to have been successful,[131] and by the 1860s Guy's Directory could claim that Queenstown's 'salubrity and equibility of climate cause it to be much frequented by valetudinarians and summer visitors'.[132] They could stay at The Queen's Hotel (centre background) where hot and cold fresh and salt water baths were provided. When the hotel opened in March 1885 it also boasted two coffee rooms, forty sitting and sleeping rooms, and a billiards room.[133] It is unlikely that the young marines striding along the pavement on the right would have entered what was then a rather select establishment.

75. THE PROMENADE

'The business portion of the town, including the best hotels and shops, faces the quay. The scene here is generally lively, what with man-o'-war's men, yachtsmen, merchant seamen, and pleasure-seekers. The promenade is a narrow asphalted enclosure, with bandstand and seats. The Band Promenades (usually on Thursdays, 7.00 to 10.00) are very popular functions.'[134] (See also page 5)

Guide to Cork & the Southwest of Ireland, 1903

76. SCOTT'S SQUARE

Queenstown, like most other Irish towns at this period, was traditional in its politics and while loyalties split over such issues as Home Rule, there seems to have been little division in regard to those on the socialist fringe of Irish political life. While James Connolly and a few supporters from the dockyards attempted to hold public meetings in the town in March 1911, the Urban District Council refused them the use of a room in the Town Hall, the building to the left of the arch. Attempts to hold a public meeting in Scott's Square, now Casement Square, were even less successful, and Connolly and his supporters had to take refuge in the bar of the Rob Roy Hotel after being attacked on the evening of Tuesday, 7 March.[135] The trouble had started after a 'rather squeaking voice yelled out: what about free love? Tell it all to us.'[136] Connolly was knocked from his soapbox as the mob charged to cries of 'up de Mollies'.[137] He was escorted by police to the Rob Roy and only managed to leave after a shower of rain dispersed his antagonists. Further meetings proved to be equally unsuccessful.

77. ROB ROY HOTEL

78. THE 'EMIGRANTS HOME'

The 'Emigrants Home' on West Beach has had a varied and fascinating history. It was at one time the Club House of the Royal Cork Yacht Club and when they moved into their new premises at Westbourne Place (see page 106), the Queenstown Yacht Club took over.[139] The next tenant was Miss Grace O'Brien, the daughter of William Smith O'Brien of abortive 1848 fame. She opened it as an 'Emigrants Home', as many of the emigrants passing through the port were not treated very well. Some idea of the conditions at the time can be obtained from a Government inquiry in the early 1880s. One report found that 'four or five men are sometimes put into one bed' and another told of musicians who were employed to rouse the emigrants who had gone to bed, so that when they joined in the festivities their places could be taken by others. Efforts to have the lodging-house clauses of the Public Health (Ireland) Act 1878 put into force met with 'active opposition' from the Town Commissioners, and the clauses were not adopted until 1881. The worst half dozen or so lodging-houses were situated on 'the Rock'; the remainder being private houses which only opened for the emigrant season.[139] Unfortunately, Miss O'Brien's Emigrants Home does not seem to have been very successful, and the building later became a 'Soldiers' Home and Sailors' Rest'.

79. WHALEBOATS

The double-ended whaleboats lying on the slip alongside the former offices of the Cork Harbour Commissioners (right) were built in the style of a whaling ship's lifeboat. Their narrow bow-shaped stern enabled them to cope well in heavy seas. They were used for a variety of purposes by a wide range of people, from ships agents and merchants, to harbour pilots and fishermen. The shopkeepers of the

town, in particular the drapers, also kept whaleboats with a 'water-clerk' and crew so as to get orders from ships arriving off the coast. The *Cork Examiner,* after reporting 'another of those shocking disasters' in September 1884, called for legislation which would prohibit the boats from venturing too far beyond the seaward limits of the harbour. Six men had drowned a few miles off Galley Head 'through persevering in foolhardiness at the bidding of their employers'.[140]

The boat lying nearest the cart belonged to the Harbour Commissioners and was used by the men who went out to tend the buoys in the harbour.[141]

80. HARBOUR ROW

Miss Burke's Pub at 3 Harbour Row probably looked much the same when Jack Doyle, 'The Gorgeous Gael', was refused a job there washing glasses and stacking bottles in the mid-1920s. Apparently Miss Burke took one look at the ungainly youngster and refused to believe that he was a mere twelve years old. He later enlisted in the Irish Guards, where he made his name as a boxer, before turning professional in 1932. In little more than a year, however, he had become a highly paid singer, having been disqualified from boxing for six months after a controversial fight with the reigning British champion, Jack Peterson. In 1935 he finally abandoned boxing and went on to feature in a number of films. The former boxer and entertainer is now buried in Cobh.[142]

The delivery cart outside the pub would seem to be ready to pull away, as the ramp for rolling down the barrels is turned back to keep the remaining two barrels in place.

81. SAILORS' HOME

From 1856 the sailors of the Royal Navy could get accommodation in the 'Royal Sailors' Home' in Harbour Row (above). In later years, Elise Sandes ran a 'Soldiers' Home and Sailors' Rest' on West Beach (see page 111). This latter home was well positioned opposite the landing stage on West Beach where soldiers and sailors came ashore, unlike her earlier 'cramped little dwelling' which does not seem to have been so conveniently located. A distraught Miss Sandes opened her first 'Soldiers' Home' in Cork in June 1877 after she discovered that no respectable lodging-house in the city would accept soldiers. Realising 'something of the fearful — almost irresistible — temptations which beset our soldiers outside Barracks', she 'longed to have some safe place of resort for them, where, instead of being dragged down to hell, they would be led up to God'.[143] By the turn of the century her Homes stretched from Queenstown to Belfast and to such outposts of the Empire as Rawal Pindi and Ranikhet.

82. WEST VIEW

The town's most picturesque mid-nineteenth century terrace is situated at West View (foreground) where the houses, known as the 'pack of cards', climb up the slope from Casement Square (formerly Scott's Square) to the 'top of the hill'. Belvedere Terrace (right background) was gradually acquired by the Mercy Nuns, who originally established themselves in Nos. 1 and 2 in May 1850. By 1870 the nuns were running an industrial school which catered for young boys and girls up to the age of sixteen. The orphanage which they had opened at Belvedere Terrace was later transferred to Rushbrooke where it became known as the Greenwich School, because it was subscribed to by the Royal Navy.[144] The large mid-nineteenth century house on the left is the residence of the Catholic Bishop of Cloyne.

CONVENT SCHOOL. QUEENSTOWN. 3897. W.L.

83. CONVENT SCHOOL

The Mercy Nuns at Belvedere Terrace ran a school where they taught 'industrial and art needlework' to the girls in their care. The girls in the centre of this photograph are threading frames which will later be placed in the looms on either side of the room. Their work seems to have been of a high quality for the *Cork Examiner* favourably reported an exhibition in December 1891 where 'the linen for ladies costumes was, as regards material, colour and finish, equal to the best that could be turned out in Belfast or Manchester'.[145] At that time the looms had only been at work for a short period and they were being mainly used for weaving fine linen, particularly cambric handkerchiefs.

84. ST. COLMAN'S CATHEDRAL

This spectacular French-Gothic cathedral was designed by Edward Welby Pugin and the Cork architect, George Coppinger Ashlin. Though the foundation stone was formally laid by Bishop William Keane in September 1868, the building was not completed until 1915 by which time Pugin was long dead (1875) and Thomas Coleman had become Ashlin's partner. The first Mass was celebrated in the newly-roofed cathedral by Bishop John McCarthy on the 15 June 1879 but due to lack of funds further building work was interrupted from 1883 to 1889. Bishop Robert Browne, who completed the work of his two predecessors, had the old Bridewell which faced the west entrance removed. The height of the roof of the nave and transepts is 100 feet and the completed tower, where a magnificent carillon of bells was installed in May 1916, now soars to a dizzy pinnacle of 287 feet.[146] Admiralty House can be seen away on the hillside to the left and the tower of St. Mary's, Church of Ireland, is on the right.

85. QUEENSTOWN STATION

The Queenstown branch of the Cork and Youghal Direct Railway was opened in March 1862. Though the line ran directly to Cork, the terminus was at Summerhill. A through connection to the Great Southern & Western Railway terminus at Lower Glanmire Road was not provided until 1868. The Cork Youghal and Queenstown Company appears to have been unsuccessful for by this time it had been bought out by the GS & WR for about half its original cost. Local trains continued to use Summerhill station till the mid-1890s, while trains going to Dublin went through Glanmire.[147] Signs for both stations can be seen on the left.

86. QUEENSTOWN STATION

From the 1860s on, most of the young men and women setting off for America would have arrived in Queenstown by train. Cork experienced a greater intensity of emigration than any other Irish county during the second half of the nineteenth century, and even when H.V. Morton visited Cobh in the 1920s it still seemed to him 'the saddest spot in Ireland'.[148] The great majority of emigrants were young, landless labourers and servants who had no prospects at home. Both Cunard and the White Star Line had special jetties along West Beach where outgoing passengers took tenders to the vessels waiting near the harbour entrance. One of the Clyde Shipping Company's tenders is shown moored at Deepwater Quay above, where generally only incoming passengers landed. The Customs Offices were in the station.

87. ADMIRALTY HOUSE

The Edwardian admiralty base[149] in Cork harbour was, in the words of one naval officer, 'a nice pleasant station unaccustomed to violent excitements, a kind of Service back-water right away from the world's turmoil and most convenient if you happened to enjoy outdoor sports'. Not surprisingly 'it was not usually sought for by the most ambitious officers'. For the officers who were stationed there, the town itself seems to have had little attraction. In their opinion, it was nothing more than a 'somewhat dull main thoroughfare of second-rate shops, inferior hotels, a long shipping quay and the Royal Cork Yacht Clubhouse'.[150]

Above the town and commanding a splendid position overlooking the harbour stood Admiralty House, which was erected in the mid-1880s. The verandahs on its south side are typical of nineteenth century colonial architecture and examples of this type of design can be found as far away as Hong Kong. The house was burnt in 1923. It was rebuilt in 1928 by the Bishop of Cloyne, Dr. Browne, as a noviciate for the Convents of Mercy in the Cloyne diocese.

ADMIRALTY YACHT. QUEENSTOWN. 4803. W.L.

88. ADMIRALTY YACHT

The Admiralty Yacht was traditionally named 'Enchantress'. This particular ship was a 3,470 ton, 320 foot, purpose-built yacht which was launched at Belfast in November 1903. She served as a hospital ship during the First World War and as a yacht in peace-time until she was finally scrapped in 1935.[151]

89. HMS 'REVENGE'

The 'Revenge' was built at Pembroke Dock and was launched on 16 April 1859. However, she had not been completed before the launch of the armoured HMS 'Warrior' rendered all 'wooden walls' obsolete. In 1867, the Revenge had the indignity to founder at Daunts Rock at the harbour entrance when she was sent to intercept the 'Erin's Hope' which had sailed from New York carrying arms for the Fenians.[152] (As the rebellion had already been suppressed, however, the Erin's Hope returned to America without landing.) Five years later, in August 1872, the Revenge became the stationery base ship at Queenstown and remained there until she was renamed 'Empress' in 1890 and towed to the Clyde. Under her new name she served as a training ship and was not broken up until 1924.[153]

Spike Island, in the background, served as a convict depot from 1847 until 1883. There is a description by Canon Sheehan, a curate of St. Colman's Cathedral (1881-89), of 'the long row of prisoners .... in the unmistakable grey jackets and with the unmistakable shuffling step . . . moving slowly across the bridge that connected Spike and Haulbowline'.[154] The bridge was erected in 1867, the year of rebellion, so that prisoners could be used in the building of a new naval basin and dry dock at Haulbowline. It was removed in the mid-1890s.[155]

90. HMS 'HOWE'

The 'Howe' served as port guardship from 1897 to 1901. She had previously served in the Mediterranean and Channel fleets and had been stranded at Ferrol on 8 December 1892. She was one of a series of vessels known as the Admiral Class; each bore the name of a distinguished British admiral. All were constructed with a pear-shaped barbette at each end for one or two heavyguns and had a broadside battery of six-inch guns between the barbettes. The ship's armour plating did not extend to the ends and was apparently the object of some criticism.[156] On the other hand, a speed of seventeen knots was a considerable improvement on earlier vessels. The Howe was built at Pembroke and was launched on 28 April 1885. She was sold by the Admiralty in 1921.

The yachts nearest the Howe seem to be the Cork Harbour One Design Class. The bowsprit and gib were added to the original rigging around 1900.[157]

91. WHITEPOINT SLIP

For all its modesty, the 12-oar naval cutter at Whitepoint Slip is suggestive of the breezy assuredness which gave the navy a special place in the hearts of all 'right thinking Englishmen'. As one officer unblushingly remembered it, the navy's job 'was to safeguard law and order throughout the world — safeguard civilization, put out fires onshore, and act as guide, philosopher and friend to the merchant ships of all nations'.[158] The fruits of that civilization can be seen on the hillside behind where a series of splendid semi-Ds vie with one another in rival Italianate and Gothic styles. This sort of housing is one of the most characteristic products of the Victorian period and reflects the tastes of the nouveau, and not-so-nouveau, riche who came to live at Midleton Park, on the western edge of Queenstown, from the mid-century onwards.

Chapter 8
The Harbour Villages

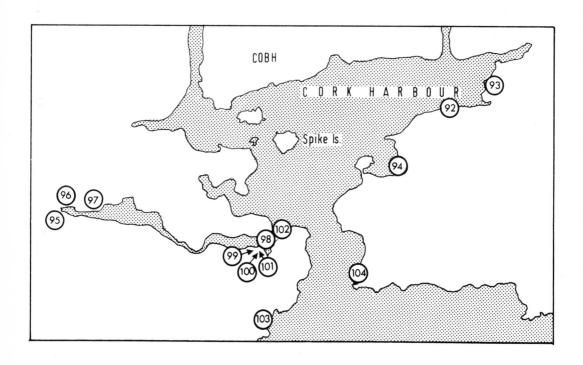

92. AGHADA

In Aghada, as in many other Irish villages, the small shop often doubled-up as a pub, with the groceries sold from one counter and spirits from the other. The demarcation is neatly indicated at Bride's (left) where the fascia-board is clearly divided into three sections, with the signs for the 'Store' and the 'Spirits' separated by the name of the proprietor. The sign between the first floor windows is for Beamish & Crawford's porter and stout. P. F. Martin's on the right has some finely lettered advertisements for Guinness's XX stout and Bass's ale as well as Cork and Dublin whiskey. The letters were shadowed to give a three-dimensional impression, which looks particularly effective from a distance.

The paddle-steamers undoubtedly brought some business to the village since Aghada was the disembarkation point for tourists going to see the round tower at Cloyne. The Cork, Blackrock and Passage Railway had a 'station-master' in Aghada to look after its interests, especially as it had a goods depot in the village from 1892; with a tramway running from the wharf to the stores. Coaches ran from there to Cloyne, Midleton, Whitegate, and Ballycotton, making Aghada the hub of a minor transport network which extended the influence of the railway company right into east Cork.[159]

93. ROSTELLAN CASTLE

The house shown here was probably built before 1750 by William, the 4th Earl of Inchiquin, who inherited the original castle from his more notorious fore-bear, Murrough O'Brien, better known as 'Murrough of the Burnings'. Murrough, the first Earl, had captured Rostellan from his kinswoman, Mrs. Fitzgerald, in 1645. His descendants seem to have followed more civilised pursuits and are best remembered for their membership in the 'Water Club' (founded 1720) which later became the Royal Cork Yacht Club. Tradition has it that an old woman cursed the Inchiquins for removing the gravestones of her family in order to pave a new kitchen; the failure of a direct Inchiquin heir to succeed another at Rostellan was thus accounted for.[160] In 1855 the last male heir died, and the property passed through a number of hands before it was finally bought by the Land Commission. The house lay empty for some years until it was demolished, along with its nineteenth century Gothic wing, in 1944.

94. WHITEGATE

Whitegate lies in a small bay on the south side of the harbour, a few miles to the southwest of Aghada. In 1861 there were about 100 houses in the village, many of them occupied by fishermen. Though at one stage Whitegate seems to have been noted for rope making, by the 1860s crochet work had taken its place as it had done 'in a hundred other villages throughout the region'.[161] Things have changed quite a lot since then, and Whitegate is now known for its neighbouring oil refinery. The building of the refinery in the early 1950s was part of a more general trend; since the Second World War the harbour has become the catalyst for large-scale industrial development in the region, with major port industries scattered at various points along the shore.

It is interesting to see how fashions have changed in the intervening years. What is perhaps most noticeable in this photograph is the number of children who are wearing caps.

95. CARRIGALINE

It was through this village that 'the united men of Carrigaline and Crosshaven marched 500 strong'[162] in August 1881 to draw attention to their claim for better agricultural wages and living conditions. Though the wages of Cork agricultural labourers had almost doubled since the Famine — mainly due to a shortage of labour as many had already emigrated — labourers still suffered from a number of grievances, in particular bad housing and irregular work. In the summer of 1881 a series of strikes occurred throughout the County as labourers voiced their belief they should share the benefit of the rent abatement farmers had recently won from the landlords. The labourers' agitation, however, gradually receded into the background as the bitter land war between the farmers and landlords got under way. The labourers, who benefited little from the great land reforms that followed, are now almost forgotten.

CARRIGALINE. Co. CORK. 9515. W.L.

96. CARRIGALINE STATION

Carrigaline was unique for a narrow-gauge station in that it had a subway which connected one platform with the other. The Cork, Blackrock and Passage Railway originally stopped at Passage but when a decision was made to extend the line to Crosshaven, the original 5'3" gauge was replaced by a narrower 3' gauge. The journey from Cork to Crosshaven took fifty minutes with stops at Blackrock, Rochestown, Passage, Glenbrook, Monkstown, Raffeen, and Carrigaline. The line was closed in 1932.[163]

97. CARRIGALINE CHURCH

Carrigaline Church is a fine example of the Gothic-style churches which were much favoured by the Board of First Fruits — the body which had responsibility for Church of Ireland building up until 1833. The churches generally had a tall and slender spire which was usually flanked by a further series of pinnacles which ran along the walls of the main building. The windows were also pointed and embellished with simple tracery. Many of the Board's churches in Munster, including Carrigaline, were designed by the brothers James and George Richard Pain. Carrigaline Parish Church was built in 1828 and was enlarged in 1835 by the addition of a north transept.[164]

98. CROSSHAVEN

The first settlement at Crosshaven took its name from a Norman cross erected in honour of St. John. It was probably situated at the Point (foreground). This small village was protected by a castle which gave rise to the now little-used name of Castlepoint. By the end of the seventeenth century a new village had developed at *Bun an Tabhairne* (background) and in later years both villages became collectively known as Crosshaven. The newer village developed into a resort which by the end of the Victorian period was sufficiently well-established to require two new churches, designed by the prestigious architects Edward Welby Pugin (St. Brigid's) and William Burges (Holy Trinity).[165]

CROSSHAVEN. CO. CORK. 8854. W.L.

99. CROSSHAVEN STATION

On 30 May 1904 the Crosshaven extension to the Cork, Blackrock and Passage Railway was formally opened by the Lord Lieutenant, the Earl of Dudley. It was a development which marked the final demise of the older resort towns in the harbour, for by the end of the century both Passage and Cobh had passed their hey-day as popular venues for holidaying Corkonians; and with the extension of the railway, Crosshaven was now only a fifty-minute journey from the city. Today the resort is best-known for its being the headquarters of the Royal Cork Yacht Club; a place 'where the wealthy of Europe clad in nautical rags (their yachts speaking for their riches) stroll along the quays and into the bars as though they were in Cherbourg, Dieppe or Honfleur'.[166]

100. CROSSHAVEN PIER

The pier at which the steamer is berthed — the present 'foul berth' — was built by the Cork, Blackrock and Passage Railway Company to accommodate its steamers, popularly known as the 'green-boats'. Passengers could take the company's train from Cork to Passage where they were met by connecting steamers which serviced the lower harbour as far as Aghada and Crosshaven. Though the railway steamers successfully competed with those of the older established operators, the boats were costly to run and the company decided that it would be more profitable to extend the railway to Crosshaven. Nevertheless, the green-boats continued to play an important, if ever diminishing, role in the life of the harbour villages until their final departure when the railways amalgamated in 1925. The green boats' chief rival, the Citizens' River Steamers Company, had ceased operations in 1890.[167]

101. THE LOWER ROAD

The building on the far left was known as Knocknagore cottage and was attached to a farm called the cottage farm, belonging to Crosshaven House. The house later became a constabulary barracks and eventually ended up as a business premises. The shed behind the trees on the right was a ticket-office for the 'green-boats'.

THE BEACH.CROSSHAVEN.8858.W.L.

CASTLE POINT. CROSSHAVEN. 8859. W.L.

102. THE POINT

These cottages at the Point are attractive examples of Ireland's vernacular building tradition. The proportions of wall to roof are pleasing and the other features — the chimneys, door, and windows — appear well placed. In all of these cottages the hearth was the focal point of the house and was usually positioned at the gable end, or in the partition wall which divided the kitchen from the main bedroom. The cottages were generally one-room deep and one-storey high, though some had an attic bedroom such as the hipped roof dwelling at Myrtleville (page 138). Apart from a number of subtle variations, the cottages did not change very much from place to place. Most of the rural population — and indeed some of their urban counterparts (see page 61) — would have lived in houses such as these, until traditional building materials began to be replaced by commercially manufactured ones in the late nineteenth century. When the Coastguard Station and nearby cottages were photographed at Myrtleville around 1900 the thatch had already begun to give way to slate and galvanise. Today, both scenes have changed dramatically.

103. MYRTLEVILLE

104. ROCHES POINT

References

1. William Bulfin, *Rambles in Eireann* (1907, re-issued Dublin: Gill and Macmillan, 1979), p.359.

2. Daniel Corkery, *The Threshold of Quiet* (Dublin: Talbot Press, 1971), pp.3-4.

3. Seán O Faoláin, *Bird Alone* (1936, reissued London: Millington, 1973), pp.137-8.

4. See William O'Sullivan, *The Economic History of Cork City from the Earliest Times to the Act of Union* (Cork: Cork University Press, 1937), pp.16-42.

5. William Camden, *Britannia, 1587,* ed. P. Holland, (Oxford: Edmund Gibson, 1695), p.979.

6. Arthur Young, *A Tour of Ireland* (1780, reissued Shannon: Irish University Press, 1970), vol 1, p.332. See Eugene Carbery, 'The Development of Cork City (as shown by the maps of the city prior to the Ordnance Survey map of 1841-42)' *Journal of the Cork Historical and Archaeological Society* (Series 2), 48 (1943): 67-81.

7. Olive Cook in Micheál MacLiammóir, *Ireland* (London: Thames and Hudson, 1966), p.141.

8. See T. Crofton Croker, *The Popular Songs of Ireland* (London: Henry Colburn, 1839) p.272. The

rhyming with 'main' suggests that the contemporary Cork pronunciation of Deane was 'Dain'. The most visible part of Elizabeth Deane's work is the group of six large storehouses which can be seen as one looks over to Haulbowline from Cobh.

9. Denis Power, 'The Architecture of Cork' *Cork Our City* (Cork: Cork Museum Catalogue, 1980), p.16.

10. Alan Brien, 'Metropolis' *Punch,* 11 July 1979.

11. Queen Victoria, *Leaves from the Journal of Our Life in the Highlands from 1848 to 1861* (London: Smith Elder, 1868), p.176.

12. Engels to Marx, 27 September 1869, in L. I. Golman, ed., *Karl Marx and Frederick Engels, Ireland and the Irish Question* (Moscow: Progress Publishers, 1971), p.273.

13. Stephen Gwynn, *The Famous Cities of Ireland* (Dublin: Maunsel, 1915), p.310.

14. *Views of Cork, Blarney and Queenstown: 53 Platinatone Views with Descriptive Guide to the District,* Emerald Isle Album Series (Dublin: William Lawrence, n.d.).

15. Kieran· Hickey, *The Light of Other Days: Irish Life at the Turn of the Century in the Photographs of Robert French* (London: Allen Lane, 1973). This is the standard work on the Lawrence Collection to which I am indebted.

16. Fr. Augustine, *Footprints of Father Theobald Mathew* (Dublin: M. H. Gill, 1947).

17. 'The Boys of Fair Hill', like most traditional songs, has been adapted and added to over the years. This particular refrain is, more than likely, one of the later additions. See Tomás O Canainn, ed., *Songs of Cork* (Skerries: Gilbert Dalton, 1978), pp.34-5.

18. The trams on the other routes had different letters at each end. The Blackpool-Douglas service had B.P. (Blackpool) on the northern end (see page 17) and D.S. (Douglas-Statue) on the other; while the Tivoli-Blackrock service had T.S. on the northern end and B.S. on the other. See Walter McGrath, 'The Tramways of Cork' *The Tramway Review* 2 (1953): 63-77.

19. Richard Ellman, *James Joyce* (London: Oxford University Press, 1959), p.37.

20. Quoted in John J. Horgan, 'A Cork Centenary' *Studies* 30 (1941): 571-79. Further information is given in the paper's 125th anniversary supplement, *Cork Examiner,* 31 August 1966.

21. A vivid account of 'the sacking of Cork' is given by Florence O'Donoghue in *Rebel Cork's Fighting Story* (Tralee: Anvil Books, n.d.)

22. Letter from J. P. Jones in the *Dublin Builder* 1 (1859): 59-60.

23. *Dublin Builder* 2 (1860): 310.

24. Rev. Terence J. McKenna and Charles V. Moore, *The Modest Men of Christ Church, Cork* (Cork: privately published, 1970).

25. John Montague, 'Overlooking Cork' *Ireland of the Welcomes* 24 (1975): 20.

26. Inscription on the base of the fountain.

27. These lines are taken from a ballad on the Berwick Fountain by John Fitzgerald (1825-1910) "the bard of the Lee". See D. A. O'Shea, ed., *Legends, Ballads and Songs of the Lee* (Cork: Guy & Co., 1913), pp.156-7.

28. Bryan A. Cody tells this yarn in his book, *The River Lee Cork and The Corkonians* (1859, reissued Cork, Tower Books, 1974), p.99. Two plaques over the Grand Parade entrances state that the 'Grand Parade Buildings' were 'Erected by the Corporation of Cork, ad, 1884, Daniel Vincent Murphy esq. Mayor M. J. McMullan esq. BE. City Engineer, Mr. Terence O'Flynn, builder'.

29. *Dublin Builder* 3 (1861): 390.

30. A photograph of the statue at this position can be seen in the *Journal of the Cork Historical and Archaeological Society* (Series 2), 48 (1943): 45.

31. *Cork Examiner,* 4 and 10 March 1862.

32. Ibid., 14 March 1862.

33. Inscription on monument.

34. Trams wanting to take a short-cut in the opposite direction, from the South Mall to Patrick Street, ran along Marlborough Street. See Walter McGrath, 'The Trams that Ran Through Morgan Street' *Evening Echo,* 18 May 1978.

35. For an account of Brash's antiquarian work, see T. F. O'Sullivan, 'Richard Rolt Brash, Cork Pioneer Archaeologist's Notable Life-work' *Cork Examiner,* 13 October 1934.

36. Padraig O'Maidin, 'Sir Thomas Deane Architect', *Cork Examiner,* 31 May 1978.

37. Séamus Murphy 'The Stones of Cork' *Hollybough* (1969). The six semi-circular panels at parapet level depict navigation, agriculture, commerce, industry, and two floral works, whereas those above the first-floor windows contain the arms of the different towns in which the bank had branches.

38. *Irish Builder* 22 (1880): 99.

39. Francis Guy, *County and City of Cork Directory* (1906), pp.481, 483.

40. Florence O'Donoghue, *Tomás MacCurtain: Soldier and Patriot* (Tralee: Anvil Books, 1971), p.166.

41. Seán O Faoláin, *Vive Moi! An Autobiography* (London: Rupert Hart-Davis, 1967), p.18.

42. St. Patrick's was originally known as the Brickfield Chapel because of a brick factory near the site. P. Calahane, 'The Catholic Parish Churches of Cork' *Journal of the Cork Historical and Archaeological Society* 48 (1943): 29.

43. In 1968 a firm of consultants made a number of extravagant proposals for traffic improvements within the city which would have left both churches isolated at either side of an alarmingly 'sinuous and spaghetti-like' road junction. For an idea of how this might have looked, see Peter Dovell, *An Environmental Study of Cork* (Dublin: An Foras Forbartha, 1971), pp.39-41.

44. *Cork Constitution,* 2 August 1861. See also, John O'Shea, 'The Non-Conformist Communities of Cork city' *Journal of the Cork Historical and Archaeological Society* 48 (1943): 40.

45. *Irish Builder* 33 (1891): 73, and *Cork Examiner,* 2 February 1893.

46. However, the pediment and pilasters were removed and the alignment of the steps altered around 1901.·

47. Sylvester O'Sullivan, ·'An Epic of Bridges' *Evening Echo,* 9 July 1975.

48. *Dublin Builder* 3 (1861): 390.

49. See the list of works attributed to Deane, Son & Woodward in Frederick O'Dwyer's and Jeremy William's essay on 'Benjamin Woodward' in Tom Kennedy, ed., *Victorian Dublin* (Dublin: Albertine Kennedy, 1980), p.59.

50. Inscription on pulpit.

51. Quoted in Fr. Bernard Curran's *Guide to St. Mary's Dominican Church, Cork* (Cork: privately published, n.d.), p.15.

52. *Shaw's Tourists Picturesque Guide to Killarney & Cork* (London: Ward Lock & Co., 1881), p.19.

53. *Historical Guide* (Cork: Crawford Municipal School of Art, 1966).

54. Sylvester Sullivan, 'Proud Day for City at Opening of Athenaeum' *Evening Echo*, 18 June 1975.

55. Séamus Murphy, *Stone Mad* (London: Routledge and Kegan Paul, 1966), p.157.

56. William J. Barry, 'History of port of Cork Steam Navigation, 1815-1915' *Journal of the Cork Historical and Archaeological Society* (Series 2), 23 (1918): 196-97.

57. Walter McGrath, 'Tomorrow is 65th Anniversary of Brian Boru and Clontarf Bridges' *Evening Echo*, 31 December 1976.

58. William J. Barry, op. cit., p.199.

59. Emmet Larkin, *James Larkin, Irish Labour Leader 1876-1947* (London: Routledge and Kegan Paul, 1965), pp.54-5.

60. Edmund Spenser, *The Faerie Queene,* ed. A. C. Hamilton, (London: Longman, 1977), p.516. The city which Spenser described lay further upstream between the North and South Gate Bridges.

61. I am very grateful to Mr. Tony McNamara for this information.

62. The exhibition halls were subsequently offered to the Royal Cork Institution.

63. John Francis Maguire, *The Industrial Movement in Ireland as illustrated by the National Exhibition of 1852* (Cork: John O'Brien, 1853), pp.17, 149.

64. *Irish Builder* 29 (1887): 144-45 and 33 (1891): 92-3.

65. Conor Cruise-O'Brien, *Parnell and his Party, 1880-90* (Oxford: Clarendon Press, 1957), p.54.

66. I am grateful to Lloyds Register of Shipping for this information.

67. I am very grateful to Mr. Tony McNamara for this information.

68. The 'Committee of the Father Mathew Centenary Celebration, Cork', invited competitive designs for a new facade to the church in the summer of 1889. Of the twelve sets submitted, the consulting architect, G. C. Ashlin, recommended a design by Walter G. Doolin as being the most suitable. However, the committee opted for the local man, D. J. Coakley, instead. See the *Irish Builder* 32 (1890): 155.

69. *Dublin, Cork and South of Ireland: a Literary, Commercial and Social Review Past and Present* (London: Stratten and Stratten, 1892), p.149.

70. A Christian Brother, *A Century of Catholic Education* (Dublin: Browne and Nolan, 1916), p.17.

71. The architect may have been Richard Brash. See the *Dublin Builder* 3 (1861): 390.

72. James S. Donnelly, 'Cork Market: Its Role in the Nineteenth Century Irish Butter Trade' *Studica Hibernica* 11 (1971): 130-63.

73. I am very grateful to Mr. Tony McNamara for this information.

74. *Irish Builder* 2 (1869): 153.

75. Seán Beecher, *The Story of Cork* (Cork: Mercier, 1971), p.29.

76. Jack Lynch, 'Tanora and a Motor Car with Lights' *Magill* 1 (1977): 59.

77. B. M. O'Brien, 'Collins Barracks, Cork' *An Cosantoir* 25 (1965): 219-27.

78. Nora Robertson, *Crowned Harp: Memories of the Last Years of the Crown in Ireland* (Dublin: A. Figgis, 1960), p.69.

79. John O'Shea, 'The Churches of the Church of Ireland in Cork City' *Journal of the Cork Historical and Archaeological Society* (Series 2), 48 (1943): 33.

80. *Irish Builder* 14 (1873): 246.

81. Ibid., 30 (1888): 30.

82. Seán O Faoláin, *An Irish Journey* (London: Longmans, Green & Co., 1940), p.86.

83. *Irish Times,* 16 April 1970. These remarks were made by Mr. Lynch at a dinner commemorating the centenary of disestablishment.

84. *Dublin Builder* 5 (1863): 28-9.

85. Lord Macaulay, *The History of England from the Accession of James the Second,* ed. Charles Harding Firth, (London: Macmillan, 1914), vol. 3, p.1466. Macaulay also referred to the University as a 'Gothic College worthy to stand in the High Street of Oxford'.

86. David Nolan, *The County Cork Grand Jury, 1836-99* (Cork: MA thesis, University College, 1974), pp.99-101, 237-39.

87. T. F. McNamara, 'The Architecture of Cork 1700-1900' *Yearbook of the Royal Institute of the Architects of Ireland* (1960): 18-19.

88. *Guide to Cork and the South-West of Ireland* (London: Ward Lock & Co., 1903), p.41. The student population attending the college dropped from 404 in 1881-82 to 171 in 1899-1900. This trend was also mirrored in the other colleges. See F. S. Lyons, *Ireland Since the Famine* (London: Fontana, 1975), pp.93-8.

89. *Irish Builder* 21 (1879): 130.

90. Quoted in the *University College Cork Record* 52 (1977): 78.

91. *Irish Builder* 26 (1884): 159 and 28 (1886): 27.

92. James Joyce, *A Portrait of the Artist as a Young Man* (1916, reissued St. Albans: Panther Books, 1977), p.84.

93. *Cork Examiner,* 3 May 1902.

94. Ibid., 3 May 1902.

95. Ibid., 2 May 1902.

96. John O.Shea, 'The Churches of the Church of Ireland in Cork City' *Journal of the Cork Historical and Archaeological Society* (Series 2), 48 (1943): 32.

97. David Nolan, op. cit., pp.97-8, 174-5.

98. Arthur Hill, 'Architecture in Cork, 1859-1903' *Journal of the Cork Historical and Archaeological Society* (Series 2) 15 (1909): 115.

99. This comment, which accompanied a photograph of the asylum, is taken from a volume of 400 photographs of Ireland published by a Chicago firm in the 1890s, so as to make 'Ireland better known to the people of all nations'. Significantly, the firm offered to donate five percent of the profits to the Gaelic League in New York. John F. Finerty, *Ireland in Pictures* (Chicago: J. S. Hyland, c.1890), p.312.

100. J. C. (James Coleman), 'The Castles of Ballincollig and Carrigrohane, Co. Cork' *Journal of the Cork Historical and Archaeological Society* (Series 2), 16 (1910): 1-8. A more recent account of life in the castle is given by M. Jesse Hoare in *The Road to Glenanore* (London: Howard Baker, 1975).

101. A. T. Newham, *The Cork & Muskerry Light Railway*, Locomotion Papers no.39, (Lingfield: Oakwood Press, 1968).

102. John Benson, 'An account of the Skew Bridge Built on the New Western Entrance to Cork' *Transactions of the Institution of Civil Engineers of Ireland* 4 (1849-50): 1-2.

103. *Dublin University Magazine* 85 (1875): 757.

104. Clement W. Scott, *Round About the Islands* (London: Tinsley Brothers, 1874), p.44. Richard Barter (1802-70) was born at Cooldaniel, Co. Cork and qualified at the London College of Physicians. He opened his water-cure establishment at St. Anne's in 1842. See Henry Boylan, *A Dictionary of Irish Biography* (Dublin: Gill and Macmillan, 1978), p.19.

105. *Irish Builder* 12 (1870): 170.

106. The castle also featured at the Louisiana Purchase Exposition at St. Louis in 1904. See Jeanne Sheehy, *The Rediscovery of Ireland's Past: the Celtic Revival 1830-1930* (London: Thames and Hudson, 1980), pp.131-34.

107. Fr. Prout (Sylvester Mahony), 'The Groves of Blarney'. See T. Crofton Croker, op. cit., p.145.

108. Mark Girouard, *The Victorian Country House* (New Haven: Yale University Press, 1979), p.9.

109. James S. Donnelly, *The Land and People of Nineteenth-Century Cork* (London: Routledge and Kegan Paul, 1975), p.251.

110. Oscar Wilde, *The Importance of Being Earnest* (1899, reissued London: Eyre Methuen, 1966), p.17.

111. D. K. Kelleher, 'Cork Park', in *The Glamour of Cork* (Dublin: Talbot Press, 1919), p.63.

112. The last race meeting was held there on Easter Monday 1917. G.M. 'The Cork Improvement Act,

1917' *Journal of the Cork Historical and Archaeological Society* (Series 2), 23 (1917): 172-73.

113. *Ford in Ireland, the First Sixty Years* (Cork: Henry Ford, 1977), pp.10-11.

114. Frank O'Connor, *Dutch Interior* (New York: Alfred A. Knoff, 1940), p.4.

115. W. M. Thackeray, *The Irish Sketch-Book* (London: Chapman and Hall, 1843), vol. 1, p.116.

116. W. E. H. Lecky, *The Leaders of Public Opinion in Ireland* (London: Saunders, Otley & Co., 1861), p.280.

117. J. C. (James Coleman), 'The Old Castles around Cork Harbour' *Journal of the Cork Historical and Archaeological Society* (Series 2), 20 (1914): 168-75.

118. Queen Victoria, op. cit., p.177.

119. E. G. Sarsfield-Hall, *From Cork to Khartoum: Memories of Southern Ireland and the Anglo-Egyptian Sudan 1868 to 1936* (Cork: privately published, 1975), p.4.

120. These are the first two verses of 'The Groves of Glanmire'. For the rest of the song, see Tomás O Canainn, op. cit., pp.90-91.

121. Edward Malins and Patrick Bowe, *Irish Gardens and Demesnes from 1830* (London: Barrie and Jenkins, 1980), pp.69-73.

122. H. C. Brockfield, 'Cobh and Passage West' *Irish Geography* 2 (1952): 156-67. See also J. D. A. Johnson 'The Passage Docks: A Century of Progress and Decay' *Journal of the Cork Historical and Archaeological Society* (Series 2), 38 (1932): 73-82.

123. Will West, *A Directory and Picture of Cork and its Environs* (Cork, 1810), p.11.

124. Alec R. Day 'Royal Victoria Hotel and Baths' in Charlie Hennesy, ed., *Our Place* 2 (1979): 9-13.

125. *Guide to Cork and the South-West of Ireland*, op. cit., p.51.

126. Brian de Breffny and Rosemary ffolliot, *The Houses of Ireland* (London: Thames and Hudson, 1975), pp.45-8. J. C. (James Coleman) 'The Old Castles around Cork Harbour' *Journal of the Cork Historical and Archaeological Society* (Series 2), 21 (1915): 1-4.

127. *Guide to Cork and the Southwest of Ireland*, op. cit., p.54.

128. Patrick Shaffrey, 'Five Cities' in Sharon Gmelch, ed., *Irish Life* (Dublin: O'Brien Press, 1979), p.94.

129. According to William Garner, Casement Square (see page 89) 'is a copy in miniature of seafront squares in Brighton'. William Garner, *Cobh Architectural Heritage* (Dublin: An Foras Forbartha, 1979), p.1.

130. H. Donegan, *History of Yachting in the South of Ireland* (Cork: Eagle Printing Works, 1909), p.3. Gibson states that the clubhouse was built in 1854. Rev. Charles Bernard Gibson, *The History of the County and City of Cork* (London: T. C. Newby, 1861), vol. 2, p.433.

143

131. See D. H. Scott, 'The Medical Topography of Cove' in J. Windele *Guide to Cove and the Harbour of Cork* (Cork: Bolster, 1840), pp.96-106. However, one English clergyman complained that the stench 'in the front street of the Queen's Town' on St. Bartholomew's Day 1858 was so offensive that it would provide an ample field for those interested in 'nasal arithmetic'. Rev. S. R. Hole, *A little Tour in Ireland* (London: Bradbury and Evans, 1859), p.201.

132. Francis Guy, *County and City of Cork Directory* (1875-76), p.291.

133. See 'A Haven for Queens and Commodores' in *The Cobh Annual* (1978), pp.63-9.

134. *Guide to Cork and the Southwest of Ireland,* op. cit., p.55.

135. C. Desmond *Greaves, The Life and Times of James Connolly* (London: Lawrence and Wishart, 1961), p.206.

136. Quoted in a letter to the editor, *Cork Free Press,* 10 March 1911. The editions for 9 and 11 March give additional information.

137. The 'Molly Maguires' was the name given to the followers of John Redmond, the leader of the pro-Parnellite wing of the Irish Parliamentary Party. Their opponents were the 'All for Ireland' supporters of William O'Brien, a Cork city M.P. The party split over Parnell's stance in the famous Kitty O'Shea divorce case of 1890, and for many years afterwards bitter fights broke out between both groups, particularly at election time.

138. This club was formed by Captain Seymour of Willmount Castle. After it merged with the Royal Western Yacht Club, it moved to the Western's Club-house at No. 2 Westbourne Place. The Club collapsed on the death of Captain Seymour. See 'Cobh's Great Houses' *The Cobh Annual* (1777), pp.8, 11.

139. 'Reports on the State of the Lodging Houses in Queenstown' *British Parliamentary Papers* 64 (1882): 563.

140. *Cork Examiner,* 3 September 1884.

141. I am very grateful to Mr. Charles Nash for this information.

142. 'Jack Doyle: A Prince of Cobh' *The Cobh Annual* (1979), pp.5-17.

143. Elise Sandes, *Enlisted; or, My Story* (London: S. W. Partridge, 1902), p.64.

144. I am very grateful to Sr. Marcella Barry for this information.

145. *Cork Examiner,* 15 December 1891.

146. A detailed description of the building is given in Patrick Thompson's *St. Colman's Cathedral, Cobh* (Cork: Guy & Co., 1958).

147. Patrick Thompson, 'Cork — Cobh Railway is Just 100 Years Old' *Evening Echo,* 23 March 1962.

148. H. V. Morton, *In Search of Ireland* (London: Methuen, 1930), p.104.

149. The Admiralty first set up a regular naval station at 'Cove' in 1805 but this was closed at the end of the Napoleonic wars. It was only in the 1840s that the station was permanently re-established.

150. E. Keble Chatterton, *Danger Zone: The Story of the Queenstown Command* (London: Rich and Cowan, 1943), pp.16-17.

151. I am very grateful to the Naval Historical Branch of the British Ministry of Defence for this information.

152. D. N. Bruinicardi, 'The History of Haulbowline' *An Cosantoir* 25 (1965): 462.

153. According to the Naval Historical Branch of the British Ministry of Defence the 'Revenge' was built 'as a 91-gun screw 2nd Rate, of 5,260 tons, and 245 feet long'.

154. Cannon P. A. Sheehan, *The Graves of Kilmorna: A Story of '67* (London: Longmans, Green & Co., 1916), p.210.

155. Niall Brunicardi, *Haulbowline Spike and Rocky Islands in Cork Harbour* (Cork: Cork Historical Guides Committee, 1968), pp.29-33.

156. S. Eardley-Wilmot, *The Development of Navies during the Last Half-Century* (London: Seeley & Co., 1892), pp.105-06.

157. I am very grateful to Mr. Charles Nash for this information.

158. Quoted in James Morris, *Pax Britannica: The Climax of an Empire* (Harmondsworth: Penguin Books, 1979), p.424.

159. A. T. Newham, *The Cork, Blackrock & Passage Railway* Locomotion Papers No.49 (Lingfield: Oakwood Press, 1970), pp.17-18.

160. J. C. (James Coleman), 'The Old Castles around Cork Harbour' *Journal of the Cork Historical and Archaeological Society* (Series 2), 21 (1915): 167-69. See also J. C. 'Rostellan Castle and Its Owners' *JCHAS* 41 (1936): 109-11.

161. Rev. C. B. Gibson, op. cit., p.433.

162. *Cork Examiner,* 10 August 1881. An authoritative account of 'the labourers' struggle' is given by James S. Donnelly, op. cit., pp.324-42.

163. Walter McGrath, 'The Cork, Blackrock and Passage Railway' *Hollybough* (1972), pp.21-2.

164. Brian de Breffney and George Mott, *The Churches and Abbeys of Ireland* (London: Thames and Hudson, 1976), p.148.

165. Diarmuid O Murchadha, *History of Crosshaven* (Cork: Cork Historical Guides Committee, 1967).

166. Tim Pat Coogan, *The Irish: A Personal View* (London: Phaidon, 1975), p.23.

167. For further information on the 'green-boats' see D. B. McNeill, *Irish Passenger Steamship Services* (Newton Abbot: David and Charles, 1971), pp.154-62 and A. T. Newham, *The Cork Blackrock & Passage Railway,* Locomotion Papers No.49 (Lingfield: Oakwood Press, 1970).

Index

GRAND   PA